Lectionary
Advent 2015 to the eve of Advent 2016 (Year C)

Church House Publishing

Published by   Church House Publishing
Church House
Great Smith Street
London SW1P 3AZ

Compilation ©   *The Archbishops' Council 2015*

ISBN   978-0-7151-2280-8 (standard)
978-0-7151-2281-5 (large)

Authorization   The Common Worship Calendar and Lectionaries are authorized pursuant to Canon B 2 of the Canons of the Church of England for use until further resolution of the General Synod of the Church of England.

Copyright and Acknowledgements   *The Revised Common Lectionary* is copyright © The Consultation on Common Texts: 1992. The Church of England adaptations to the Principal Service Lectionary are copyright © The Archbishops' Council, as are the Second and Third Service Lectionaries, the Weekday Lectionary for Morning and Evening Prayer and the Additional Weekday Lectionary.

The Daily Eucharistic Lectionary derives, with some adaptation, from the *Ordo Lectionum Missae* of the Roman Catholic Church and is reproduced by permission of The International Commission on English in the Liturgy.

Edited by Peter Moger
Designed by Derek Birdsall & John Morgan/Omnific
Typeset by RefineCatch Ltd, Bungay, Suffolk
Printed in England by Core Publications

ontents of this booklet

s booklet gives details of the full range of
ssibilities envisaged in the liturgical calendar and
:ionary of Common Worship. Its use as a tool for
 preparation of worship will require the making of
eral choices based first on the general celebration
 he Christian year by the Church of England as a
le; second on the customary pattern of calendar
 he diocese, parish and place of worship; and third
 the pattern of services locally.

 first column comprises the Calendar of the
urch with the days of the year. Observances that
 mandatory are printed either in bold type
ndays), in **bold** type (Principal Feasts and Holy
rs) or in roman (Festivals). Optional celebrations
sser Festivals) and Commemorations are printed
rdinary roman type and *italic* type respectively.

 second column comprises (a) the readings and
ms for the Principal Service on Sundays, Principal
sts and Holy Days, and Festivals, and (b) Holy
mmunion readings and psalms for other days of
 week. On the Sundays after Trinity, the Old
tament reading and its psalm are divided into two
ller columns, indicating a choice between a
tinuous' reading week by week or a reading
ted' to the Gospel for that day.

 third column comprises (a) the Third Service
dings and psalms for Sundays, Principal Feasts and
y Days, and Festivals, and (b) the readings and
ms for weekday Morning Prayer.

 fourth column comprises (a) the Second
vice readings and psalms for Sundays, Principal
sts and Holy Days, and Festivals, and (b) the
dings and psalms for weekday Evening Prayer.

Additional Weekday Lectionary, intended
icularly for use in places of worship that attract
asional rather than daily worshippers, is provided
ages 70–77. It may be used either at Morning or
ing Prayer.

Common of the Saints

General readings and psalms for saints' days can be
found on pages 79–83; for some particular
celebrations, other readings are suggested there.

Special Occasions

Readings and psalms for special occasions can be
found on pages 84–86.

Liturgical colours

Appropriate liturgical colours are suggested in this
booklet. They are not mandatory; traditional or local
use may be followed.

Colours are indicated by single letters: the first
(always upper case) for the season or Festival; and
occasionally a second (lower case) for an optional
celebration on that day. Thus, for example, *Gr* for the
celebration of a Lesser Festival whose liturgical
colour is red, in an otherwise 'green' season.

The following abbreviations are used:

G	Green
P or p	Purple or Violet
P(La)	Purple or Lent array
R or r	Red
W or w	White (Gold is indicated where its use would be appropriate)

Notes on the Lectionary

Sundays, Principal Feasts and Holy Days and Festivals

Three sets of psalms and readings are provided for each Sunday, Principal Feast or Holy Day and Festival.

The **Principal Service lectionary** (based on the Revised Common Lectionary) is intended for use at the principal service of the day (whether this service is Holy Communion or some other authorized form). In most Church communities, this is likely to be the mid-morning service, but the minister is free to decide which service time normally constitutes the Principal Service of the day. This lectionary may be used twice if required – for example, at an early celebration of Holy Communion and then again at a later one.

If only **two readings** are used at the Principal Service and that service is Holy Communion, the second reading must always be the Gospel reading. When the Principal Service lectionary is used at a service other than Holy Communion, the Gospel reading need not always be chosen.

The **Second Service lectionary** is intended for a second main service. In many churches, this lectionary may be the appropriate provision for a Sunday afternoon or evening service. A Gospel reading is always provided so that this lectionary can, if necessary, be used where the second main service is a celebration of Holy Communion.

The **Third Service lectionary**, with shorter readings, is intended where a third set of psalms and readings is needed and is most appropriate for use at an office. A Gospel reading is not always provided, so this lectionary is not suitable for use at Holy Communion.

Weekdays

The Common Worship Weekday Lectionary authorized by the General Synod in 2005 comprises a lectionary (with psalms) for Holy Communion, a lectionary for Morning and Evening Prayer, and tables of psalms for Morning and Evening Prayer.

The **Daily Eucharistic Lectionary** (based on the Roman Catholic daily eucharistic lectionary) is a semi-continuous two-year lectionary with a wide use of scripture, though not complete coverage of the Bible. Two readings are provided for each day, the first from either the Old or New Testament, the second always a Gospel. Psalm provision is intended to be a brief response to the first reading. It is for use at Holy Communion normally in places with a daily or near-daily celebration with a regular congregation. It may also be used as an office lectionary.

The **lectionary for Morning and Evening Prayer** always provides two readings for each office, the first from the Old Testament and the second from the New Testament. These are generally in sequence. One of the New Testament readings for any particular day is from the Gospels.

The **psalms for Morning and Evening Prayer** follow a sequential pattern in Ordinary Time (apart from the period from All Saints to the beginning of Advent).

In the periods from All Saints until 18 December, from the Epiphany until the Presentation of Christ in the Temple (Candlemas), from Ash Wednesday until Palm Sunday, and from the Monday after Easter Week until Pentecost, there is a choice of psalms at Morning and Evening Prayer. The psalms printed first reflect the theme of the season. Alternatively, the psalms from the Ordinary Time cycle may be used. The two sets are separated by 'or'.

From 19 December until the Epiphany and from the Monday of Holy Week until the Saturday of Easter Week, only seasonal psalms are provided.

Where more than one psalm is given, one psalm (printed in **bold**) may be used as the sole psalm at that office.

Guidance on how these options for saying the psalms are expressed typographically can be found in the 'Notes on the Lectionary' below.

A further cycle is provided (see table on page 86) which is largely the monthly sequential cycle of psalms given in the *Book of Common Prayer*.

A single psalm for use by those who only say one office each day is provided in Prayer During the Day in *Common Worship: Daily Prayer*.

An **Additional Weekday Lectionary**, intended particularly for use in places of worship that attract occasional rather than daily worshippers, is provided on pages 70–78. It can be used either at Morning or Evening Prayer. Psalmody is not provided and should be taken from provision outlined above.

Using the Lectionary tables

Bible references (except to the Psalms) are to *New Revised Standard Version* (New York, 1989). Those who use other Bible translations should check verse numbers against the *NRSV*. Each reference gives book, chapter and verse, in that order. References to the Psalms are to the Common Worship psalter, published in *Common Worship: Services and Prayers for the Church of England* (2000) and *Common Worship: Daily Prayer* (2005). A table showing the verse number differences between this and the psalter in the *Book of Common Prayer* is provided on the Common Worship web site (http://www.churchofengland.org/prayer-worship/worship/texts/the-psalter/psalterverses.aspx).

Options in the provision of readings or psalms are presented in the following ways:
- square brackets [xx] give either optional additional verses or Psalms, or a shorter alternative;
- 'or' indicates a simple choice between two alternative readings or courses of psalms;
- a psalm printed in **bold** may be used as the sole psalm at that office;
- on weekdays a psalm printed in parentheses (xx) is omitted if it has been used as the opening canticle at that office;
- a psalm marked with an asterisk may be shortened if desired.
- Where a reading from the **Apocrypha** is offered, alternative Old Testament reading is provided.

In the choice of **readings other than the Gospel** reading, the minister should ensure that, in any year, a balance is maintained between readings in the Old and New Testaments and that, where a particular biblical book is appointed to be read over several weeks, the choice ensures that the continuity of one book is not lost.

On the Sundays after Trinity, the Principal Service Lectionary provides **alternative Old Testament readings and psalms**. References in the left-hand column (under the heading 'Continuous') offer a semi-*continuous* reading of Old Testament texts. Both a reading and its complementary psalmody stand independently of the other readings. References in the right-hand column (under the heading 'Related') *relate* the Old Testament reading and the psalm to the Gospel reading. One column should be followed for the whole sequence of Sundays after Trinity.

The Lectionary 2015–2016

Sunday and festal readings for 29 November 2015 (the First Sunday of Advent) to 26 November 2016 (the eve of Advent Sunday) are from **Year C**, which offers a semi-continuous reading of Luke's Gospel at the Principal Service on Sundays throughout the year.

The weekday readings for Holy Communion are from **Year Two** of the Daily Eucharistic Lectionary (DEL).

Office readings are from Table 2 of the Weekday Lectionary: at Morning Prayer, Old Testament 1 and New Testament 1; and, at Evening Prayer, Old Testament 2b in Ordinary Time and 2a in Seasonal Time and New Testament 2.

Notes on the Calendar 29 November 2015 — 26 November 2016

These notes are based on the Rules to Order the Christian Year (*Common Worship: Times and Seasons*, pages 24–30).

Sundays

All Sundays celebrate the paschal mystery of the death and resurrection of the Lord. They also reflect the character of the seasons in which they are set.

Principal Feasts

On these days (printed in bold) Holy Communion is celebrated in every cathedral and parish church, and this celebration, required by Canon B 14, may not be displaced by any other celebration, and may only be dispensed with in accordance with the provision of Canon B 14A.

Except in the case of Christmas Day and Easter Day, the celebration of the Feast *begins with Evening Prayer on the day before the Feast*, and the Collect at that Evening Prayer is that of the Feast. In the case of Christmas Eve and Easter Eve, there is proper liturgical provision (including a Collect) for the whole day.

The Epiphany may, for pastoral reasons, be celebrated on Sunday 3 January. **The Presentation of Christ in the Temple** (Candlemas) is celebrated on either Tuesday 2 February or Sunday 31 January. **The Annunciation of Our Lord to the Blessed Virgin Mary** (25 March), falling on Good Friday, is transferred to the Monday after the Second Sunday of Easter (4 April). **All Saints' Day** may be celebrated on Sunday 30 October (replacing the Fourth Sunday before Advent), with or without a supplementary celebration on Tuesday 1 November.

Other Principal Holy Days

These days (printed in bold), and the liturgical provision for them, may not be displaced by any other celebration.

Ash Wednesday (10 February) and **Maundy Thursday** (24 March) are Principal Holy Days. On both these days Holy Communion is celebrated in every cathedral or parish church, except where there is dispensation under Canon B 14A.

Good Friday (25 March) is a Principal Holy Day.

Eastertide

The paschal character of **the Great Fifty Days of Easter**, from Easter Day (27 March) to Pentecost (15 May), should be celebrated throughout the season, and should not be displaced by other celebrations. No Festival day may be celebrated in Easter Week; and nor may any Festival – except for a Patronal or Dedication Festival – displace the celebration of a Sunday (a memorial of the resurrection) during Eastertide. The paschal character of the season should be retained on those weekdays when saints' days are celebrated.

The three days before Ascension Day (2–4 May) are customarily observed as **Rogation Days**, when prayer is offered for God's blessing on the fruits of the earth and on human labour.

The nine days **after Ascension Day until the eve of Pentecost** (6–14 May) are observed as days of prayer and preparation for the celebration of the outpouring of the Holy Spirit.

Ordinary Time

Ordinary Time comprises two periods in the year: first, the period from the day after the Presentation of Christ in the Temple until the day before Ash Wednesday, and second, that from the day after Pentecost until the day before the First Sunday of Advent.

During Ordinary Time, there is no seasonal emphasis, except that the period between All Saints' Day and the First Sunday of Advent is a time to celebrate and reflect upon the reign of Christ in earth and heaven.

Festivals

These days (printed in roman), and the liturgical provision for them, are not usually displaced. For each day there is full liturgical provision for a Principal, Second and Third Service, and an optional so-called

First Evening Prayer on the evening before the Festival where this is required.

Festivals may not be celebrated on Sundays in Advent, Lent or Eastertide, the Baptism of Christ, Ascension Day, Trinity Sunday or Christ the King, or weekdays between Palm Sunday and the Second Sunday of Easter.

If Festivals falling on a Sunday – namely John, Apostle and Evangelist (falling on the First Sunday of Christmas) and Thomas the Apostle (falling on the Sixth Sunday after Trinity) – are transferred from that Sunday, the pattern in 2015–16 should be: John on Tuesday 29 December in 2015 and Thomas on Monday 4 July 2016.

Certain Festivals (namely, Matthias the Apostle, the Visit of the Blessed Virgin Mary to Elizabeth, Thomas the Apostle, and the Blessed Virgin Mary) have customary alternative dates (see page 8).

The Thursday after Trinity Sunday (26 May) may be observed as the **Day of Thanksgiving for the Institution of Holy Communion** (sometimes known as *Corpus Christi*), and may be kept as a Festival.

Other Celebrations

Mothering Sunday falls on the Fourth Sunday of Lent (6 March). Alternative prayers and readings are provided for the Principal Service. **Bible Sunday** may be celebrated on 23 October, replacing the Last Sunday after Trinity, and appropriate prayers and readings are provided.

Local Celebrations

The celebration of **the patron saint or the title of a church** is kept either as a Festival or as a Principal Feast.

The **Dedication Festival** of a church is the anniversary of the date of its dedication or consecration. This is kept either as a Festival or as a Principal Feast. When kept as Principal Feasts, the Patronal and Dedication Festivals may be transferred to the nearest Sunday, unless that day is already a Principal Feast or one of the following days: the First Sunday of Advent, the Baptism of Christ, the First Sunday of Lent, the Fifth Sunday of Lent, or Palm Sunday. If the actual date is not known, the Dedication Festival may be celebrated on 2 October (replacing the Nineteenth Sunday after Trinity), or 23 October (replacing the Last Sunday after Trinity), or on a suitable date chosen locally. Readings can be found on page 78.

Harvest Thanksgiving may be celebrated on a Sunday in autumn, replacing the provision for that day, provided it does not displace any Principal Feast or Festival.

iocesan and other local provision may be made in **calendar of the saints** to supplement the eral calendar, in accordance with Canon B 6, graph 5.

ser Festivals

er Festivals (printed in ordinary roman type, in k) are observed in a manner appropriate to a icular place. Each is provided with a Collect, which supersede the Collect of the week. For certain er Festivals a complete set of Eucharistic readings ovided, and for others appropriate readings may elected from the Common of the Saints (see s 79–83). These readings may, at the minister's retion, supersede the Daily Eucharistic Lectionary). The weekday psalms and readings at Morning Evening Prayer are not usually superseded by e for Lesser Festivals, but at the minister's retion psalms and readings provided on these days se at Holy Communion may be used instead at ning or Evening Prayer.

he minister may be selective in the Lesser ivals that are observed and may also keep some, l of them, as Commemorations, perhaps cially in Advent, Lent and Easter where the acter of the season ought to be sustained. If the of Thanksgiving for the Institution of Holy munion (26 May) is not kept as a Festival, it may ept as a Lesser Festival.

/hen a Lesser Festival falls on a Principal Feast or Day, a Festival, a Sunday, or on a weekday ween Palm Sunday and the Second Sunday of er, its celebration is normally omitted for that However, where there is sufficient reason, it may, e discretion of the minister, be celebrated on the est available day.

nmemorations

memorations (printed in *italic*) are made by a tion in prayers of intercession. They are not ided with Collect, Psalm and Readings, and do not ce the usual weekday provision at Holy munion or at Morning and Evening Prayer. he minister may be selective in the memorations that are made.

nly where there is an established celebration in vider Church or where the day has a special local ficance may a Commemoration be observed as a er Festival, with liturgical provision from the mon of the Saints (pages 79–83).

designating a Commemoration as a Lesser val, the minister must remember the need to tain the spirit of the season, especially of Advent, and Easter.

Days of Discipline and Self-Denial

The weekdays of Lent and every Friday in the year are days of discipline and self-denial, with the exception of Principal Feasts, Festivals outside Lent, and Fridays from Easter Day to Pentecost. The day preceding a Principal Feast may also be appropriately kept as a day of discipline and self-denial in preparation for the Feast.

Ember Days

Ember Days should be kept, under the bishop's directions, in the week before an ordination as days of prayer for those to be ordained deacon or priest.

Ember Days may also be kept even when there is no ordination in the diocese as more general days of prayer for those who serve the Church in its various ministries, both ordained and lay, and for vocations. Traditionally they have been observed on the Wednesday, Friday and Saturday in the week before the Third Sunday of Advent, the Second Sunday of Lent, and the Sundays nearest to 29 June and 29 September.

Notes on Collects

For a table showing where the Collects and Post Communions are published, see page 86.

Where a Collect ends 'through Jesus Christ … now and for ever', the minister may omit the longer (trinitarian) ending and use the shorter ending, 'through Jesus Christ our Lord', to which the people respond, 'Amen'. The longer ending, however, is to be preferred at a service of Holy Communion.

The Collect for each Sunday is used at Evening Prayer on the Saturday preceding, except where that Saturday is a Principal Feast, or a Festival, or the eve of Christmas Day or Easter Day. The Collect for each Sunday is also used on the weekdays following, except where other provision is made.

Abbreviations used in this book

Alt	Alternative	
Bp	Bishop	
BVM	Blessed Virgin Mary	
DEL	Daily Eucharistic Lectionary	
EP	Evening Prayer	
G	Green	

HC	Holy Communion: used where additional references are given to provide alternative texts for use at a celebration of Holy Communion (most often the provision of a psalm or gospel)	P or p	Purple or Violet
		P(La)	Purple or Lent Array
		Ps & Pss	Psalmody
		R or r	Red
		W or w	White (Gold is indicated where its use would be appropriate)
MP	Morning Prayer		

Standard abbreviations have been used for other books of the Bible where necessary.

Alternative dates

The following may be celebrated on the alternative dates indicated:

Matthias the Apostle
– on **25 February** instead of 14 May

The Visit of the Blessed Virgin Mary to Elizabeth
– on **2 July** instead of 31 May

The Blessed Virgin Mary
– on **8 September** instead of 15 August

If any of the three festivals is celebrated on the alternative date these provisions should be used on the principal date:

Holy Communion	Morning Prayer	Evening Prayer
If Matthias the Apostle is celebrated on Thursday 25 February the following provision is used on Saturday 14 May (W):		
Acts 28.16–20, 30–end	Psalms 42, **43** or 120, **121**, 122	1st **EP of Pentecost**
Psalm 11.4–end	Number 32.1–27	Psalm 48
John 21.20–end	Luke 9.1–17	Deuteronomy 16.9–15
	*Micah 3.1–8; Ephesians 6.10–20 (at MP only)	John 7.37–39
If The Visit of the Blessed Virgin Mary to Elizabeth is celebrated on Saturday 2 July the following provision is used on Tuesday 31 May (G):		
2 Peter 3.11–15a, 17–end	Psalms 32, **36**	Psalm **33**
Psalm 90.1–4, 10, 14, 16	Joshua 21.43—22.8	Job 14
Mark 12.13–17	Luke 12.13–21	Romans 7.7–end
If The Blessed Virgin Mary is celebrated on Thursday 8 September the following provision is used on Monday 15 August (G):		
Ezekiel 24.15–24	Psalms **98**, 99, 101	Psalm **105*** (or 103)
Psalm 78.1–8	2 Samuel 11	Proverbs 14.31—15.17
Matthew 19.16–22	Acts 8.26–end	Mark 6.45–end

8

For guidance on how the options for saying the psalms are expressed typographically, see page 5.

Sundays (and Principal Feasts, other Principal Holy Days, and Festivals)

Day	Date		Principal Service	3rd Service	2nd Service
	Sunday / Feast † / Festival ††	Colour	Main service of the day: Holy Communion, Morning Prayer, Evening Prayer, or a Service of the Word	Shorter Readings, an Office lectionary probably used at Morning Prayer where Holy Communion is the Principal Service	2nd main Service, probably used at Evening Prayer; adaptable for Holy Communion

† Principal Feasts and other Principal Holy Days are printed in bold.
†† Festivals are printed in roman typeface.

Weekdays

Day	Date		Holy Communion		Morning Prayer	Evening Prayer
		Colour	Weekday readings		Psalms and readings for Morning Prayer	Psalms and readings for Evening Prayer

‡ Lesser Festivals are printed in roman typeface, in black.
# Commemorations are printed in italics.

Lesser Festival ‡* [optional]
Commemoration ‡# [optional]

‡ Lesser Festivals are printed in roman typeface, in black.
# Commemorations are printed in italics.
* The ascriptions given to holy men and women in the Calendar (such as martyr, teacher of the faith, etc.) have often been abbreviated in this booklet for reasons of space. The particular ascription given is there to be helpful if needing to choose Collects and readings from Common of the Saints; where several ascriptions are used (e.g. bishop and martyr), traditionally the last ascription given is the most important and therefore the guiding one. The full ascriptions may be found in the Calendar, which is printed in Common Worship: Times and Seasons (pages 7–22), Common Worship: Festivals (pages 5–20) and Common Worship: Daily Prayer (pages 5–16). These incorporate minor corrections made since the publication of the Calendar in Common Worship: Services and Prayers for the Church of England (pages 5–16).

	Principal Service	3rd Service	2nd Service
Sunday 29 November P **1st Sunday of Advent**	Jeremiah 33.14–16 Psalm 25.1–9 1 Thessalonians 3.9–end Luke 21.25–36	Psalm 44 Isaiah 51.4–11 Romans 13.11–end	Psalm 9 [or 9.1–8] Joel 3.9–end Revelation 14.13—15.4 HC John 3.1–17 *or:* 1st EP of Andrew the Apostle: Psalm 48; Isaiah 49.1–9a; 1 Corinthians 4.9–16
Monday 30 November R Andrew the Apostle	Isaiah 52.7–10 Psalm 19.1–6 Romans 10.12–18 Matthew 4.18–22	MP Psalms 47, 147.1–12 Ezekiel 47.1–12 or Ecclesiasticus 14.20–end John 12.20–32	EP Psalms 87, 96 Zechariah 8.20–end John 1.35–42
	Holy Communion	**Morning Prayer**	**Evening Prayer**
Tuesday 1 December P *Charles de Foucauld, hermit, 1916*	Isaiah 11.1–10 Psalm 72.1–4, 18–19 Luke 10.21–24	Psalms **80**, 82 or **5**, 6 (8) Isaiah 26.1–13 Matthew 12.22–37	Psalms **74**, 75 or **9**, 10* Isaiah 43.1–13 Revelation 20
Wednesday 2 December P	Isaiah 25.6–10a Psalm 23 Matthew 15.29–37	Psalms 5, **7** or 119.1–32 Isaiah 28.1–13 Matthew 12.38–end	Psalms 76, **77** or 11, 12, 13 Isaiah 43.14–end Revelation 21.1–8
Thursday 3 December P *Francis Xavier, missionary, 1552*	Isaiah 26.1–6 Psalm 118.18–27a Matthew 7.21, 24–27	Psalms **42**, 43 or 14, **15**, 16 Isaiah 28.14–end Matthew 13.1–23	Psalms **40**, 46 or **18*** Isaiah 44.1–8 Revelation 21.9–21
Friday 4 December P *John of Damascus, monk,* *teacher of the faith, c.749* *Nicholas Ferrar, deacon, founder of* *the Little Gidding Community, 1637*	Isaiah 29.17–end Psalm 27.1–4, 16–17 Matthew 9.27–31	Psalms **25**, 26 or 17, **19** Isaiah 29.1–14 Matthew 13.24–43	Psalms 16, **17** or **22** Isaiah 44.9–23 Revelation 21.22—22.5
Saturday 5 December P	Isaiah 30.19–21, 23–26 Psalm 146.4–9 Matthew 9.35—10.1, 6–8	Psalms **9** (10) or 20, 21, **23** Isaiah 29.15–end Matthew 13.44–end	Psalms **27**, 28 or **24**, 25 Isaiah 44.24—45.13 Revelation 22.6–end

			Principal Service	3rd Service	2nd Service
			Holy Communion	Morning Prayer	Evening Prayer
Sunday	6 December 2nd Sunday of Advent	P	Baruch 5 or Malachi 3.1–4 Canticle: Benedictus Philippians 1.3–11 Luke 3.1–6	Psalm 80 Isaiah 64.1–7 Matthew 11.2–11	Psalms 75 [76] Isaiah 40.1–11 Luke 1.1–25
Monday	7 December Ambrose, bishop, teacher of the faith, 397 (see p. 80)	Pw	Isaiah 35 Psalm 85.7–end Luke 5.17–26	Psalm 44 or 27, 30 Isaiah 30.1–18 Matthew 14.1–12	Psalms 144, 146 or 26, 28, 29 Isaiah 45.14–end 1 Thessalonians 1
Tuesday	8 December Conception of the Blessed Virgin Mary (see p. 79)	Pw	Isaiah 40.1–11 Psalm 96.1, 10–end Matthew 18.12–14	Psalms 56, 57 or 32, 36 Isaiah 30.19–end Matthew 14.13–end	Psalms 11, 12, 13 or 33 Isaiah 46 1 Thessalonians 2.1–12
Wednesday	9 December Ember Day	P	Isaiah 40.25–end Psalm 103.8–13 Matthew 11.28–end	Psalms 62, 63 or 34 Isaiah 31 Matthew 15.1–20	Psalms 10, 14 or 119.33–56 Isaiah 47 1 Thessalonians 2.13–end
Thursday	10 December Ember Day	P	Isaiah 41.13–20 Psalm 145.1, 8–13 Matthew 11.11–15	Psalms 53, 54, 60 or 37* Isaiah 32 Matthew 15.21–28	Psalm 73 or 39, 40 Isaiah 48.1–11 1 Thessalonians 3
Friday	11 December Ember Day	P	Isaiah 48.17–19 Psalm 1 Matthew 11.16–19	Psalms 85, 86 or 31 Isaiah 33.1–22 Matthew 15.29–end	Psalms 82, 90 or 35 Isaiah 48.12–end 1 Thessalonians 4.1–12
Saturday	12 December Ember Day	P	Ecclesiasticus 48.1–4, 9–11 or 2 Kings 2.9–12 Psalm 80.1–4, 18–19 Matthew 17.10–13	Psalm 145 or 41, 42, 43 Isaiah 35 Matthew 16.1–12	Psalms 93, 94 or 45, 46 Isaiah 49.1–13 1 Thessalonians 4.13–end

		Principal Service	3rd Service	2nd Service
Sunday	13 December 3rd Sunday of Advent	P Zephaniah 3.14–end Canticle: Isaiah 12.2–end [or Psalm 146.4–end] Philippians 4.4–7 Luke 3.7–18	Psalms 12, 14 Isaiah 25.1–9 1 Corinthians 4.1–5	Psalms 50.1–6 [62] Isaiah 35 Luke 1.57–66 [67–80]
		Holy Communion	**Morning Prayer**	**Evening Prayer**
Monday	14 December John of the Cross, poet, teacher of the faith, 1591 (see p. 80)	Pw Numbers 24.2–7, 15–17 Psalm 25.3–8 Matthew 21.23–27	Psalm **40** or 44 Isaiah 38.1–8, 21–22 Matthew 16.13–end	Psalms 25, **26** or **47**, 49 Isaiah 49.14–25 1 Thessalonians 5.1–11
Tuesday	15 December	P	Zephaniah 3.1–2, 9–13 Psalm 34.1–6, 21–22 Matthew 21.28–32	Psalms 70, 74 or **48**, 52 Isaiah 38.9–20 Matthew 17.1–13	Psalms **50**, 54 or **50** Isaiah 50 1 Thessalonians 5.12–end
Wednesday	16 December	P	Isaiah 45.6b–8, 18, 21b–end Psalm 85.7–end Luke 7.18b–23	Psalms **75**, 96 or 1**19.57–80** Isaiah 39 Matthew 17.14–21	Psalms 25, **82** or **59**, 60 (67) Isaiah 51.1–8 2 Thessalonians 1
Thursday	17 December *O Sapientia* Eglantyne Jebb, social reformer, founder of 'Save The Children', 1928	P	Genesis 49.2, 8–10 Psalm 72.1–5, 18–19 Matthew 1.1–17	Psalms **76**, 97 or 56, **57** (63*) Zephaniah 1.1–2.3 Matthew 17.22–end	Psalms 44 or 61, **62**, 64 Isaiah 51.9–16 2 Thessalonians 2
Friday	18 December	P	Jeremiah 23.5–8 Psalm 72.1–2, 12–13, 18–end Matthew 1.18–24	Psalms 77, **98** or **51**, 54 Zephaniah 3.1–13 Matthew 18.1–20	Psalm **49** or **38** Isaiah 51.17–end 2 Thessalonians 3
Saturday	19 December	P	Judges 13.2–7, 24–end Psalm 71.3–8 Luke 1.5–25	*From Saturday 19 December until the Epiphany* *the seasonal psalmody must be used at Morning and Evening Prayer.* Psalms 144, **146** Zephaniah 3.14–end Matthew 18.21–end	Psalms 10, **57** Isaiah 52.1–12 Jude

	Principal Service	3rd Service	2nd Service
Sunday 20 December 4th Sunday of Advent *P*	Micah 5.2–5a Canticle: Magnificat or Psalm 80.1–8 Hebrews 10.5–10 Luke 1.39–45 [46–55]	Psalm 144 Isaiah 32.1–8 Revelation 22.6–end	Psalms 123 [131] Isaiah 10.33—11.10 Matthew 1.18–end
	Holy Communion	**Morning Prayer**	**Evening Prayer**
Monday 21 December *P*	Zephaniah 3.14–18 Psalm 33.1–4, 11–12, 20–end Luke 1.39–45	Psalms 121, 122, 123 Malachi 1.1, 6–end Matthew 19.1–12	Psalms 80, 84 Isaiah 52.13–end of 53 2 Peter 1.1–15
Tuesday 22 December *P*	1 Samuel 1.24–end Psalm 113 Luke 1.46–56	Psalms 124, 125, 126, 127 Malachi 2.1–16 Matthew 19.13–15	Psalms 24, 48 Isaiah 54 2 Peter 1.16—2.3
Wednesday 23 December *P*	Malachi 3.1–4, 4.5–end Psalm 25.3–9 Luke 1.57–66	Psalms 128, 129, 130, 131 Malachi 2.17—3.12 Matthew 19.16–end	Psalm 89.1–37 Isaiah 55 2 Peter 2.4–end
Thursday 24 December Christmas Eve *P*	*Morning Eucharist only:* 2 Samuel 7.1–5, 8–11, 16 Psalm 89.2, 19–27 Acts 13.16–26 Luke 1.67–79	Psalms 45, 113 Malachi 3.13–end of 4 Matthew 23.1–12	Psalm 85 Zechariah 2 Revelation 1.1–8
Friday 25 December Christmas Day *Gold or W*	Any of the following three sets of Principal Service readings may be used on the evening of Christmas Eve and on Christmas Day. Set III should be used at some service during the celebration. **Set I** Isaiah 9.2–7 Psalm 96 Titus 2.11–14 Luke 2.1–14 [15–20] **Set II** Isaiah 62.6–end Psalm 97 Titus 3.4–7 Luke 2.[1–7] 8–20 **Set III** Isaiah 52.7–10 Psalm 98 Hebrews 1.1–4 [5–12] John 1.1–14	MP Psalms 110, 117 Isaiah 62.1–5 Matthew 1.18–end	*EP* Psalm 8 Isaiah 65.17–25 Philippians 2.5–11 or Luke 2.1–20 *if it has not been used at the principal service of the day*
Saturday 26 December Stephen, deacon, first martyr *R*	2 Chronicles 24.20–22 or Acts 7.51–end Psalm 119.161–168 Acts 7.51–end or Galatians 2.16b–20 Matthew 10.17–22	MP Psalms 13, 31.1–8, 150 Jeremiah 26.12–15 Acts 6	EP Psalms 57, 86 Genesis 4.1–10 Matthew 23.34–end

13

John / Christmas 1

		Principal Service	3rd Service	2nd Service
Sunday	**27 December** W John, Apostle and Evangelist	Exodus 33.7–11a Psalm 117 1 John 1 John 21.19b–end	*MP* Psalms **21**, 147.13–end Exodus 33.12–end 1 John 2.1–11	*EP* Psalm **97** Isaiah 6.1–8 1 John 5.1–12

Or, if John is transferred to 29 December:

		Principal Service	3rd Service	2nd Service
Monday	**28 December** R The Holy Innocents	Jeremiah 31.15–17 Psalm 124 1 Corinthians 1.26–29 Matthew 2.13–18	*MP* Psalms **36**, 146 Baruch 4.21–27 or Genesis 37.13–20 Matthew 18.1–10	*EP* Psalms 123, **128** Isaiah 49.14–25 Mark 10.13–16

		Holy Communion	Morning Prayer	Evening Prayer
Tuesday	**29 December** Wr Thomas Becket, archbishop, martyr, 1170 (see p. 79)	1 John 2.3–11 Psalm 96.1–4 Luke 2.22–35	Psalms **19**, 20 Jonah 1 Colossians 1.1–14	Psalms 131, **132** Isaiah 57.15–end John 1.1–18

Or, if John is transferred to 29 December:

		Principal Service	3rd Service	2nd Service
Sunday	**27 December** W **1st Sunday of Christmas**	1 Samuel 2.18–20, 26 Psalm 148 [or 148.7–end] Colossians 3.12–17 Luke 2.41–end	Psalm 105.1–11 Isaiah 41.21—42.1 1 John 1.1–7	Psalm 132 Isaiah 61 Galatians 3.27—4.7 *HC* Luke 2.15–21

		Principal Service	3rd Service	2nd Service
Monday	**28 December** The Holy Innocents	Jeremiah 31.15–17 Psalm 124 1 Corinthians 1.26–29 Matthew 2.13–18	*MP* Psalms **36**, 146 Baruch 4.21–27 or Genesis 37.13–20 Matthew 18.1–10	*EP* Psalms 123, **128** Isaiah 49.14–25 Mark 10.13–16
Tuesday	**29 December** W John, Apostle and Evangelist	Exodus 33.7–11a Psalm 117 1 John 1 John 21.19b–end	*MP* Psalms **21**, 147.13–end Exodus 33.12–end 1 John 2.1–11	*EP* Psalm **97** Isaiah 6.1–8 1 John 5.1–12

14

		Holy Communion	Morning Prayer	Evening Prayer
Wednesday	**30 December**	W	1 John 2.12–17 Psalm 96.7–10 Luke 2.36–40	Psalms 111, 112, 113 Jonah 2 Colossians 1.15–23	Psalms **65**, 84 Isaiah 59.1–15a John 1.1–28
Thursday	**31 December** *John Wyclif, reformer, 1384*	W	1 John 2.18–21 Psalm 96.1, 11–end John 1.1–18	Psalm **102** Jonah 3–4 Colossians 1.24—2.7	Psalms **90**, 148 Isaiah 59.15b–end John 1.29–34 *or:* 1st EP of the Naming and Circumcision of Jesus: Psalm 148; Jeremiah 23.1–6; Colossians 2.8–15

		Principal Service	3rd Service	2nd Service
Friday	**1 January** Naming and Circumcision of Jesus	W	Numbers 6.22–end Psalm 8 Galatians 4.4–7 Luke 2.15–21	MP Psalms **103**, 150 Genesis 17.1–13 Romans 2.17–end	EP Psalm **115** Deuteronomy 30. [1–10] 11–end Acts 3.1–16

If the Epiphany is celebrated on Wednesday 6 January:

		Holy Communion	Morning Prayer	Evening Prayer
Saturday	**2 January** Basil the Great and Gregory of Nazianzus, bishops, teachers of the faith, 379 and 389 (see p. 80) *Seraphim, monk, spiritual guide, 1833* *Vedanayagam Samuel Azariah,* *bishop, evangelist, 1945*	W	1 John 2.22–28 Psalm **98**.1–4 John 1.19–28	Psalm **18**.1–30 Ruth 1 Colossians 2.8–end	Psalms 45, **46** Isaiah 60.1–12 John 1.35–42

If the Epiphany is celebrated on Sunday 3 January:

		Holy Communion	Morning Prayer	Evening Prayer
Saturday	**2 January** Basil the Great and Gregory of Nazianzus, bishops, teachers of the faith, 379 and 389 (see p. 80) *Seraphim, monk, spiritual guide, 1833* *Vedanayagam Samuel Azariah,* *bishop, evangelist, 1945*	W	1 John 2.22–28 Psalm **98**.1–4 John 1.19–28	Psalm **18**.1–30 Ruth 1 Colossians 2.8–end	**1st EP of the Epiphany:** Psalms **96**, 97 Isaiah 49.1–13 John 4.7–26

Christmas 2 / Epiphany

If the Epiphany is celebrated on Wednesday 6 January:

		Principal Service	3rd Service	2nd Service
Sunday 3 January **2nd Sunday of Christmas**	W	Jeremiah 31.7–14 Psalm 147.13–end	Psalm 87 Isaiah 12 1 Thessalonians 2.1–8	Psalm 135 [or 135.1–14] 1 Samuel 1.20–end 1 John 4.7–16
		or: Ecclesiasticus 24.1–12 *Canticle:* Wisdom of Solomon 10.15–end Ephesians 1.3–14 John 1.[1–9] 10–18		HC Matthew 2.13–end
		Holy Communion	**Morning Prayer**	**Evening Prayer**
Monday 4 January	W	1 John 3.7–10 Psalm 98.1,8–end John 1.35–42	Psalm 89.1–37 Ruth 3 Colossians 3.12—4.1	Psalms 85. 87 Isaiah 61 John 2.1–12
Tuesday 5 January	W	1 John 3.11–21 Psalm 100 John 1.43–end	Psalms 8, 48 Ruth 4.1–17 Colossians 4.2–end	**1st EP of the Epiphany:** Psalms 96, 97 Isaiah 49.1–13 John 4.7–26
		Principal Service	**3rd Service**	**2nd Service**
Wednesday 6 January **Epiphany**	Gold or W	Isaiah 60.1–6 Psalm 72. [1–9] 10–15 Ephesians 3.1–12 Matthew 2.1–12	MP Psalms **132**, 113 Jeremiah 31.7–14 John 1.29–34	EP Psalms **98**, 100 Baruch 4.36—end of 5 *or* Isaiah 60.1–9 John 2.1–11
		Holy Communion	**Morning Prayer**	**Evening Prayer**
Thursday 7 January	W	1 John 3.22—4.6 Psalm 2.7–end Matthew 4.12–17, 23–end	Psalms **99**, 147.1–12 *or* **78**.1–39* Baruch 1.15—2.10 *or* Jeremiah 23.1–8 Matthew 20.1–16	Psalm 118 *or* **78**.40–end* Isaiah 63.7–end 1 John 3
Friday 8 January	W	1 John 4.7–10 Psalm 72.1–8 Mark 6.34–44	Psalms **46**, 147.13–end *or* **55** Baruch 2.11–end *or* Jeremiah 30.1–17 Matthew 20.17–28	Psalm 145 *or* **69** Isaiah 64 1 John 4.7–end
Saturday 9 January	W	1 John 4.11–18 Psalm 72.1, 10–13 Mark 6.45–52	Psalms **2**, 148 *or* **76**, 79 Baruch 3.1–8 *or* Jeremiah 30.18—31.9 Matthew 20.29–end	Psalms **67**, 72 *or* 81, **84** Isaiah 65.1–16 1 John 5.1–12 *or:* 1st EP of the Baptism of Christ: Psalm 36; Isaiah 61; Titus 2.11–14; 3.4–7

		Principal Service	3rd Service	2nd Service
Sunday **3 January** Epiphany	*Gold or W*	Isaiah 60.1-6 Psalm 72. [1–9] 10–15 Ephesians 3.1–12 Matthew 2.1–12	MP Psalms **132**, 113 Jeremiah 31.7–14 John 1.29–34	EP Psalms **98**, 100 Baruch 4.36—end of 5 or Isaiah 60.1–9 John 2.1–11
		Holy Communion	*Morning Prayer*	*Evening Prayer*
Monday 4 January	W	1 John 3.22—4.6 Psalm 2.7–end Matthew 4.12–17, 23–end	Psalm 89.1–37 or 71 Ruth 2 Colossians 3.1–11	Psalms 85, 87 or **72**, 75 Isaiah 60.13–end John 1.43–end
Tuesday 5 January	W	1 John 4.7–10 Psalm 72.1–8 Mark 6.34–44	Psalms 8, 48 or 73 Ruth 3 Colossians 3.12—4.1	Psalms 96, **97** or 74 Isaiah 61 John 2.1–12
Wednesday 6 January	W	1 John 4.11–18 Psalm 72.1, 10–13 Mark 6.45–52	Psalms 127, 128, 131 or **77** Ruth 4.1–17 Colossians 4.2–end	Psalms 2, 110 or **119.81–104** Isaiah 62 John 2.13–end
Thursday 7 January	W	1 John 4.19—5.4 Psalm 72.1, 17–end Luke 4.14–22	Psalms **99**, 147.1–12 or **78.1–39*** Baruch 1.15—2.10 or Jeremiah 23.1–8 Matthew 20.1–16	Psalm 118 or **78.40–end*** Isaiah 63.7–end 1 John 3
Friday 8 January	W	1 John 5.5–13 Psalm 147.13–end Luke 5.12–16	Psalms **46**, 147.13–end or **55** Baruch 2.11–end or Jeremiah 30.1–17 Matthew 20.17–28	Psalm 145 or 69 Isaiah 64 1 John 4.7–end
Saturday 9 January	W	1 John 5.14–end Psalm 149.1–5 John 3.22–30	Psalms 2, **148** or 76, 79 Baruch 3.1–8 or Jeremiah 30.18—31.9 Matthew 20.29–end	Psalms **67**, 72 or 81, **84** Isaiah 65.1–16 1 John 5.1–12 or: 1st EP of the Baptism of Christ: Psalm 36; Isaiah 61; Titus 2.1–14; 3.4–7

17

Baptism of Christ (Epiphany 1)

			Principal Service	3rd Service	2nd Service
Sunday	**10 January** **Baptism of Christ** *1st Sunday of Epiphany*	*Gold or* W	Isaiah 43.1–7 Psalm 29 Acts 8.14–17 Luke 3.15–17, 21–22	Psalm 89.19–29 Isaiah 42.1–9 Acts 19.1–7	Psalms 46, 47 Isaiah 55.1–11 Romans 6.1–11 HC Mark 1.4–11
			Holy Communion	**Morning Prayer**	**Evening Prayer**
Monday	**11 January** *Mary Slessor, missionary, 1915* DEL week 1	W	1 Samuel 1.1–8 Psalm 116.10–15 Mark 1.14–20	Psalms **2**, 110 or 80, **82** Genesis 1.1–19 Matthew 21.1–17	Psalms **34**, 36 or 85, 86 Amos 1 1 Corinthians 1.1–17
Tuesday	**12 January** Aelred, abbot, 1167 (see p. 82) *Benedict Biscop, scholar, 689*	W	1 Samuel 1.9–20 *Canticle:* 1 Samuel 2.1, 4–8 *or* Magnificat Mark 1.21–28	Psalms 8, **9** or 87, **89.1–18** Genesis 1.20—2.3 Matthew 21.18–32	Psalms **45**, 46 or **89.19–end** Amos 2 1 Corinthians 1.18–end
Wednesday	**13 January** Hilary, bishop, teacher of the faith, 367 (see p. 80) *Kentigern (Mungo), missionary bishop, 603* *George Fox, founder of* *the Society of Friends (Quakers), 1691*	W	1 Samuel 3.1–10, 19–20 Psalm 40.1–4, 7–10 Mark 1.29–39	Psalms 19, **20** or 119.**105–128** Genesis 2.4–end Matthew 21.33–end	Psalms **47**, 48 or 91, 93 Amos 3 1 Corinthians 2
Thursday	**14 January**	W	1 Samuel 4.1–11 Psalm 44.10–15, 24–25 Mark 1.40–end	Psalms 21, 24 or 90, **92** Genesis 3 Matthew 22.1–14	Psalms **61**, 65 or **94** Amos 4 1 Corinthians 3
Friday	**15 January**	W	1 Samuel 8.4–7, 10–end Psalm 89.15–18 Mark 2.1–12	Psalms **67**, 72 or **88** (95) Genesis 4.1–16, 25–26 Matthew 22.15–33	Psalm **68** or **102** Amos 5.1–17 1 Corinthians 4
Saturday	**16 January**	W	1 Samuel 9.1–4, 17–19, 10.1a Psalm 21.1–6 Mark 2.13–17	Psalms 29, **33** or 96, **97**, 100 Genesis 6.1–10 Matthew 22.34–end	Psalms 84, **85** or **104** Amos 5.18–end 1 Corinthians 5

Day		Principal Service	2nd Service
Sunday	**17 January** W **2nd Sunday of Epiphany**	Isaiah 62.1–5 Psalm 36.5–10 1 Corinthians 12.1–11 John 2.1–11	Psalm 96 1 Samuel 3.1–20 Ephesians 4.1–16 HC John 1.29–42

		Holy Communion	**Morning Prayer**	**Evening Prayer**
Monday	**18 January** W **Week of Prayer for Christian Unity: 18–25 January** *Amy Carmichael, founder of the Dohnavur Fellowship, spiritual writer, 1951* DEL week 2	1 Samuel 15.16–23 Psalm 50.8–10, 16–17, 24 Mark 2.18–22	Psalms 145, **146** or **98**, 99, 101 Genesis 6.11–7.10 Matthew 24.1–14	Psalm 71 or 105* (or 103) Amos 6 1 Corinthians 6.1–11
Tuesday	**19 January** W *Wulfstan, bishop, 1095 (see p.81)*	1 Samuel 16.1–13 Psalm 89.19–27 Mark 2.23–end	Psalms **132**, 147.1–12 or 106* (or 103) Genesis 7.11–end Matthew 24.15–28	Psalm **89**.1–37 or **107*** Amos 7 1 Corinthians 6.12–end
Wednesday	**20 January** W *Richard Rolle, spiritual writer, 1349*	1 Samuel 17.32–33, 37, 40–51 Psalm 144.1–2, 9–10 Mark 3.1–6	Psalms **81**, 147.13–end or 110, **111**, 112 Genesis 8.1–14 Matthew 24.29–end	Psalms **97**, 98 or **119**.129–152 Amos 8 1 Corinthians 7.1–24
Thursday	**21 January** Wr *Agnes, child martyr, 304 (see p.79)*	1 Samuel 18.6–9, 19.1–7 Psalm 56.1–2, 8–end Mark 3.7–12	Psalms **76**, 148 or 113, **115** Genesis 8.15–9.7 Matthew 25.1–13	Psalms 99, 100, **111** or 114, **116**, 117 Amos 9 1 Corinthians 7.25–end
Friday	**22 January** W *Vincent of Saragossa, deacon, martyr, 304*	1 Samuel 24.3–22*a* Psalm 57.1–2, 8–end Mark 3.13–19	Psalms **27**, 149 or **139** Genesis 9.8–19 Matthew 25.14–30	Psalm **73** or 130, 131, 137 Hosea 1.1—2.1 1 Corinthians 8
Saturday	**23 January** W	2 Samuel 1.1–4, 11–12, 17–19, 23–end Psalm 80.1–6 Mark 3.20–21	Psalms **122**, 128, 150 or 120, **121**, 122 Genesis 11.1–9 Matthew 25.31–end	Psalms 61, 66 or **118** Hosea 2.2–17 1 Corinthians 9.1–14

Epiphany 3

	Principal Service	3rd Service	2nd Service
Sunday 24 January W **3rd Sunday of Epiphany**	Nehemiah 8.1–3, 5–6, 8–10 Psalm 19 [or 19.1–6] 1 Corinthians 12.12–31a Luke 4.14–21	Psalm 113 Deuteronomy 30.11–15 3 John 1.5–8	Psalm 33 [or 33.1–12] Numbers 9.15–end 1 Corinthians 7.17–24 HC Mark 1.21–28 or: 1st EP of the Conversion of Paul: Psalm 149; Isaiah 49.1–13; Acts 22.3–16
Monday 25 January W Conversion of Paul	Jeremiah 1.4–10 or Acts 9.1–22 Psalm 67 Acts 9.1–22 or Galatians 1.11–16a Matthew 19.27–end	MP Psalms 66, 147.13–end Ezekiel 3.22–end Philippians 3.1–14	EP Psalm 119.41–56 Ecclesiasticus 39.1–10 or Isaiah 56.1–8 Colossians 1.24—2.7
	Holy Communion	**Morning Prayer**	**Evening Prayer**
Tuesday 26 January W Timothy and Titus, companions of Paul DEL week 3	2 Samuel 6.12–15, 17–19 Psalm 24.7–end Mark 3.31–end *Lesser Festival eucharistic lectionary:* Isaiah 61.1–3a; Psalm 100; 1 Timothy 2.1–8 or Titus 1.1–5; Luke 10.1–9	Psalms 34, **36** or (134,) **135** Genesis 13.2–end Matthew 26.17–35	Psalm **145** or (134,) **135** Hosea 4.1–16 1 Corinthians 10.1–13
Wednesday 27 January W	2 Samuel 7.4–17 Psalm 89.19–27 Mark 4.1–20	Psalms 45, **46** or **119.153—end** Genesis 14 Matthew 26.36–46	Psalms 21, **29** or **136** Hosea 5.1–7 1 Corinthians 10.14—11.1
Thursday 28 January W Thomas Aquinas, priest, philosopher, teacher of the faith, 1274 (see p. 80)	2 Samuel 7.18–19, 24–end Psalm 132.1–5, 11–15 Mark 4.21–25	Psalms 47, 48 or **143**, 146 Genesis 15 Matthew 26.47–56	Psalms 24, 33 or **138**, 140, 141 Hosea 5.8—6.6 1 Corinthians 11.2–16
Friday 29 January W	2 Samuel 11.1–10, 13–17 Psalm 51.1–6, 9 Mark 4.26–34	Psalms 61, **65** or 142, **144** Genesis 16 Matthew 26.57–end	Psalms 67, 77 or **145** Hosea 6.7—7.2 1 Corinthians 11.17–end

		Holy Communion	Morning Prayer	Evening Prayer
Saturday	**30 January** Wr Charles, king and martyr, 1649 (see p. 79)	2 Samuel 12.1-7, 10-17 Psalm 51.11-16 Mark 4.35-end	Psalm **68** or **147** Genesis 17.1-22 Matthew 27.1-10	Psalms **72**, 76 or **148**, 149, 150 Hosea 8 1 Corinthians 12.1-11
Sunday	**31 January**　W **4th Sunday of Epiphany**	*Principal Service* Ezekiel 43.27—44.4 Psalm 48 1 Corinthians 13 Luke 2.22-40	*3rd Service* Psalm 71.1-6, 15-17 Micah 6.1-8 1 Corinthians 6.12-end	*2nd Service* Psalm 34 [or 34.1-10] 1 Chronicles 29.6-19 Acts 7.44-50 *HC* John 4.19-29a
Monday	**1 February**　W DEL week 4 *Brigid, abbess, c.525*	*Holy Communion* 2 Samuel 15.13-14, 30, 16.5-13 Psalm 3 Mark 5.1-20	*Morning Prayer* Psalms **57**, 96 or 1, 2, 3 Genesis 18.1-15 Matthew 27.11-26	*Evening Prayer* 1st **EP of the Presentation:** Psalm 118 1 Samuel 1.19b-end Hebrews 4.11-end
Tuesday	**2 February**　*Gold or W* **Presentation of Christ in the Temple** (Candlemas)	*Principal Service* Malachi 3.1-5 Psalm 24. [1-6] 7-end Hebrews 2.14-end Luke 2.22-40	*3rd Service* *MP* Psalms **48**, 146 Exodus 13.1-16 Romans 12.1-5	*2nd Service* *EP* Psalms 122, **132** Haggai 2.1-9 John 2.18-22

Presentation / Epiphany 4

If the Presentation of Christ is transferred to Sunday 31 January:

	Holy Communion	Morning Prayer	Evening Prayer
			1st EP of the Presentation:
Saturday **30 January** Charles, king and martyr, 1649 (see p. 79) *Wr*	2 Samuel 12.1–7, 10–17 Psalm 51.11–16 Mark 4.35–end	Psalm **68** or **147** Genesis 17.1–22 Matthew 27.1–10	Psalm 118 1 Samuel 1.19b–end Hebrews 4.11–end
	Principal Service	**3rd Service**	**2nd Service**
Sunday **31 January** Presentation of Christ in the Temple (Candlemas) *Gold or W*	Malachi 3.1–5 Psalm 24. [1–6] 7–end Hebrews 2.14–end Luke 2.22–40	MP Psalms **48**, 146 Exodus 13.1–16 Romans 12.1–5	EP Psalms 122, **132** Haggai 2.1–9 John 2.18–22
	Holy Communion	**Morning Prayer**	**Evening Prayer**
Monday **1 February** *Brigid, abbess, c.525* DEL week 4 Ordinary Time begins today (if the Presentation of Christ was celebrated on 31 January). The Collect of 5 before Lent is used. *G*	2 Samuel 15.13–14, 30, 16.5–13 Psalm 3 Mark 5.1–20	Psalms **1**, 2, 3 Genesis 18.1–15 Matthew 27.11–26	Psalms **4**, 7 Hosea 9 1 Corinthians 12.12–end
Tuesday **2 February** *G*	2 Samuel 18.9–10, 14, 24–25, 30—19.3 Psalm 86.1–6 Mark 5.21–end	Psalms **5**, 6 (8) Genesis 18.16–end Matthew 27.27–44	Psalms **9**, 10* Hosea 10 1 Corinthians 13

Wednesday 3 February Anskar, archbishop, missionary, 865 (see p. 82) DEL week 4 Ordinary Time begins today (if the Presentation of Christ was celebrated on 2 February). The Collect of 5 before Lent is used. Gw	2 Samuel 24.2, 9–17 Psalm 32.1–8 Mark 6.1–6a	Psalm 119.1–32 Genesis 19.1–3, 12–29 Matthew 27.45–56	Psalms 11, 12, 13 Hosea 11.1–11 1 Corinthians 14.1–19
Thursday 4 February *Gilbert, founder of the Gilbertine Order, 1189* G	1 Kings 2.1–4, 10–12 *Canticle:* 1 Chronicles 29.10–12 or Psalm 145.1–5 Mark 6.7–13	Psalms 14, 15, 16 Genesis 21.1–21 Matthew 27.57–end	Psalm 18* Hosea 11.12—end of 12 1 Corinthians 14.20–end
Friday 5 February G	Ecclesiasticus 47.2–11 Psalm 18.31–36, 50–end Mark 6.14–29	Psalms 17, 19 Genesis 22.1–19 Matthew 28.1–15	Psalm 22 Hosea 13.1–14 1 Corinthians 16.1–9
Saturday 6 February *Martyrs of Japan, 1597* Accession of Queen Elizabeth II, 1952 (see p. 85) G	1 Kings 3.4–13 Psalm 119.9–16 Mark 6.30–34	Psalms 20, 21, 23 Genesis 23 Matthew 28.16–end	Psalms 24, 25 Hosea 14 1 Corinthians 16.10–end

Sunday next before Lent

			Principal Service	3rd Service	2nd Service
Sunday	**7 February** **Sunday next before Lent**	G	Exodus 34.29–end Psalm 99 2 Corinthians 3.12—4.2 Luke 9.28–36 [37–43a]	Psalm 2 Exodus 33.17–end 1 John 3.1–3	Psalm 89.1–18 [or 89.5–12] Exodus 3.1–6 John 12.27–36a
			Holy Communion	*Morning Prayer*	*Evening Prayer*
Monday	**8 February** DEL week 5	G	1 Kings 8.1–7, 9–13 Psalm 132.1–9 Mark 6.53–end	Psalms 27, **30** Genesis 37.1–11 Galatians 1	Psalms 26, **28**, 29 Jeremiah 1 John 3.1–21
Tuesday	**9 February**	G	1 Kings 8.22–23, 27–30 Psalm 84.1–10 Mark 7.1–13	Psalms 32, **36** Genesis 37.12–end Galatians 2.1–10	Psalm 33 Jeremiah 2.1–13 John 3.22–end
			Principal Service	*3rd Service*	*2nd Service*
Wednesday	**10 February** **Ash Wednesday**	P(La)	Joel 2.1–2, 12–17 or Isaiah 58.1–12 Psalm 51.1–18 2 Corinthians 5.20b—6.10 Matthew 6.1–6, 16–21 or John 8.1–11	*MP* Psalm 38 Daniel 9.3–6, 17–19 1 Timothy 6.6–19	*EP* Psalm 51 or 102 [or 102.1–18] Isaiah 1.10–18 Luke 15.11–end
			Holy Communion	*Morning Prayer*	*Evening Prayer*
Thursday	**11 February**	P(La)	Deuteronomy 30.15–end Psalm 1 Luke 9.22–25	Psalm **77** or 37* Genesis 39 Galatians 2.11–end	Psalm **74** or 39, **40** Jeremiah 2.14–32 John 4.1–26
Friday	**12 February**	P(La)	Isaiah 58.1–9a Psalm 51.1–5, 17–18 Matthew 9.14–15	Psalms **3**, 7 or **31** Genesis 40 Galatians 3.1–14	Psalm 31 or **35** Jeremiah 3.6–22 John 4.27–42
Saturday	**13 February**	P(La)	Isaiah 58.9b–end Psalm 86.1–7 Luke 5.27–32	Psalm **71** or 41, **42**, 43 Genesis 41.1–24 Galatians 3.15–22	Psalm **73** or 45, **46** Jeremiah 4.1–18 John 4.43–end

		Principal Service	3rd Service	2nd Service
Sunday	**14 February** **1st Sunday of Lent** P(La)	Deuteronomy 26.1–11 Psalm 91.1–2, 9–end [or 91.1–11] Romans 10.8b–13 Luke 4.1–13	Psalm 50.1–15 Micah 6.1–8 Luke 5.27–end	Psalm 119.73–88 Jonah 3 Luke 18.9–14
		Holy Communion	**Morning Prayer**	**Evening Prayer**
Monday	**15 February** P(La) Sigfrid, bishop, 1045 Thomas Bray, priest, founder of SPCK and SPG, 1730	Leviticus 19.1–2, 11–18 Psalm 19.7–end Matthew 25.31–end	Psalms 10, 11 or 44 Genesis 41.25–45 Galatians 3.23—4.7	Psalms 12, **13**, 14 or **47**, 49 Jeremiah 4.19–end John 5.1–18
Tuesday	**16 February** P(La)	Isaiah 55.10–11 Psalm 34.4–6, 21–22 Matthew 6.7–15	Psalm **44** or **48**, 52 Genesis 41.46—42.5 Galatians 4.8–20	Psalms 46, **49** or **50** Jeremiah 5.1–19 John 5.19–29
Wednesday	**17 February** P(La)r Janani Luwum, archbishop, martyr, 1977 (see p. 79) Ember Day	Jonah 3 Psalm 51.1–5, 17–18 Luke 11.29–32	Psalm **6**, 17 or 119.**57–80** Genesis 42.6–17 Galatians 4.21—5.1	Psalms 9, **28** or **59**, 50, (67) Jeremiah 5.20–end John 5.30–end
Thursday	**18 February** P(La)	Esther 14.1–5, 12–14 or Isaiah 55.6–9 Psalm 138 Matthew 7.7–12	Psalms **42**, 43 or 56, **57** (63*) Genesis 42.18–28 Galatians 5.2–15	Psalms 137,138, **142** or 61, **62**, 64 Jeremiah 6.9–21 John 6.1–15
Friday	**19 February** P(La) Ember Day	Ezekiel 18.21–28 Psalm 130 Matthew 5.20–26	Psalm **22** or **51**, 54 Genesis 42.29–end Galatians 5.16–end	Psalms 54, **55** or **38** Jeremiah 6.22–27 John 6.16–27
Saturday	**20 February** P(La) Ember Day	Deuteronomy 26.16–end Psalm 119.1–8 Matthew 5.43–end	Psalms 59, **63** or **68** Genesis 43.1–15 Galatians 6	Psalms **4**, 16 or 65, **66** Jeremiah 7.1–20 John 6.27–40

25

		Principal Service	3rd Service	2nd Service
Sunday	**21 February** *P(La)* **2nd Sunday of Lent**	Genesis 15.1–12, 17–18 Psalm 27 Philippians 3.17—4.1 Luke 13.31–end	Psalm 119.161–end Genesis 17.1–7, 15–16 Romans 11.13–24	Psalm 135 [or 135.1–14] Jeremiah 22.1–9, 13–17 Luke 14.27–33
		Holy Communion	**Morning Prayer**	**Evening Prayer**
Monday	**22 February** *P(La)*	Daniel 9.4–10 Psalm 79.8–9, 12, 14 Luke 6.36–38	Psalms 26, **32** or **71** Genesis 43.16–end Hebrews 1	Psalms 70, **74** or **72**, 75 Jeremiah 7.21–end John 6.41–51
Tuesday	**23 February** *P(La)r* Polycarp, bishop, martyr, c.155 (see p. 79)	Isaiah 1.10, 16–20 Psalm 50.8, 16–end Matthew 23.1–12	Psalm **50** or **73** Genesis 44.1–17 Hebrews 2.1–9	Psalms **52**, 53, 54 or **74** Jeremiah 8.1–15 John 6.52–59
Wednesday	**24 February** *P(La)*	Jeremiah 18.18–20 Psalm 31.4–5, 14–18 Matthew 20.17–28	Psalm **35** or **77** Genesis 44.18–end Hebrews 2.10–end	Psalms **3**, 51 or **119.81–104** Jeremiah 8.18—9.11 John 6.60–end
Thursday	**25 February** *P(La)*	Jeremiah 17.5–10 Psalm 1 Luke 16.19–end	Psalm **34** or **78.1–39*** Genesis 45.1–15 Hebrews 3.1–6	Psalm **71** or **78.40–end*** Jeremiah 9.12–24 John 7.1–13
Friday	**26 February** *P(La)*	Genesis 37.3–4, 12–13, 17–28 Psalm 105.16–22 Matthew 21.33–43, 45–46	Psalms 40, **41** or **55** Genesis 45.16–end Hebrews 3.7–end	Psalms **6**, 38 or **69** Jeremiah 10.1–16 John 7.14–24
Saturday	**27 February** *P(La)w* George Herbert, priest, poet, 1633 (see p. 81)	Micah 7.14–15, 18–20 Psalm 103.1–4, 9–12 Luke 15.1–3, 11–end	Psalms 3, **25** or **76**, 79 Genesis 46.1–7, 28–end Hebrews 4.1–13	Psalms **23**, 27 or 81, **84** Jeremiah 10.17–24 John 7.25–36

		Principal Service	3rd Service	2nd Service
Sunday	**28 February** **3rd Sunday of Lent** P(La)	Isaiah 55.1–9 Psalm 63.1–9 1 Corinthians 10.1–13 Luke 13.1–9	Psalms 26, 28 Deuteronomy 6.4–9 John 17.1a,11b–19	Psalms 12, 13 Genesis 28.10–19a John 1.35–end

		Holy Communion	Morning Prayer	Evening Prayer

The following readings may replace those provided for Holy Communion on any day during the Third Week of Lent:
Exodus 17.1–7; Psalm 95.1–2, 6–end; John 4.5–42

		Holy Communion	Morning Prayer	Evening Prayer
Monday	**29 February** P(La)	2 Kings 5.1–15 Psalms 42.1–2, 43.1–4 Luke 4.24–30	Psalms **5**, 7 or 80, **82** Genesis 47.1–27 Hebrews 4.14—5.10	Psalms 11, **17** or **85**, 86 Jeremiah 11.1–17 John 7.37–52
Tuesday	**1 March** P(La)w David, bishop, patron of Wales, c.601 (see p.81)	Song of the Three 2, 11–20 or Daniel 2.20–23 Psalm 25.3–10 Matthew 18.21–end	Psalms **6**, 9 or 87, **89.1–18** Genesis 47.28—end of 48 Hebrews 5.11—6.12	Psalms 61, 62, **64** or **89.19–end** Jeremiah 11.18—12.6 John 7.53—8.11
Wednesday	**2 March** P(La)w Chad, bishop, missionary, 672 (see p. 82)	Deuteronomy 4.1, 5–9 Psalm 147.13–end Matthew 5.17–19	Psalm **38** or 119.105–128 Genesis 49.1–32 Hebrews 6.13–end	Psalms 36, **39** or 91, **93** Jeremiah 13.1–11 John 8.12–30
Thursday	**3 March** P(La)	Jeremiah 7.23–28 Psalm 95.1–2, 6–end Luke 11.14–23	Psalms **56**, 57 or 90, **92** Genesis 49.33—end of 50 Hebrews 7.1–10	Psalms **59**, 60 or 94 Jeremiah 14 John 8.31–47
Friday	**4 March** P(La)	Hosea 14 Psalm 81.6–10, 13, 16 Mark 12.28–34	Psalm **22** or 88 (95) Exodus 1.1–14 Hebrews 7.11–end	Psalm **69** or 102 Jeremiah 15.10–end John 8.48–end
Saturday	**5 March** P(La)	Hosea 5.15—6.6 Psalm 51.1–2, 17–end Luke 18.9–14	Psalm **31** or 96, **97**, 100 Exodus 1.22—2.10 Hebrews 8	Psalms 116, **130** or 104 Jeremiah 16.10—17.4 John 9.1–17

Lent 4

	Principal Service	3rd Service	2nd Service
Sunday 6 March 4th Sunday of Lent — P(La)	Joshua 5.9–12 Psalm 32 2 Corinthians 5.16–end Luke 15.1–3,11b–32	Psalms 84, 85 Genesis 37.3–4, 12–end 1 Peter 2.16–end	Psalm 30 Prayer of Manasseh or Isaiah 40.27—41.13 2 Timothy 4.1–18 HC John 11.17–44

For Mothering Sunday:
Exodus 2.1–10 or 1 Samuel 1.20–end; Psalm 34.11–20 or 127.1–4;
2 Corinthians 1.3–7 or Colossians 3.12–17; Luke 2.33–35 or John 19.25b–27
If the Principal Service readings have been displaced by Mothering Sunday provisions, they may be used at the Second Service.

	Holy Communion	Morning Prayer	Evening Prayer
	The following readings may replace those provided for Holy Communion on any day during the Fourth Week of Lent: Micah 7.7–9; Psalm 27.1, 9–10, 16–17; John 9		
Monday 7 March — P(La)r Perpetua, Felicity and companions, martyrs, 203 (see p. 79)	Isaiah 65.17–21 Psalm 30.1–5, 8, 11–end John 4.43–end	Psalms 70, 77 or 98, 99, 101 Exodus 2.11–22 Hebrews 9.1–14	Psalms **25**, 28 or **105*** (or 103) Jeremiah 17.5–18 John 9.18–end
Tuesday 8 March — P(La)w Edward King, bishop, 1910 (see p. 81) Felix, bishop, 647 Geoffrey Studdert Kennedy, priest, poet, 1929	Ezekiel 47.1–9, 12 Psalm 46.1–8 John 5.1–3, 5–16	Psalms 54, **79** or **106*** (or 103) Exodus 2.23—3.20 Hebrews 9.15–end	Psalms **80**, 82 or **107*** Jeremiah 18.1–12 John 10.1–10
Wednesday 9 March — P(La)	Isaiah 49.8–15 Psalm 145.8–18 John 5.17–30	Psalms 63, **90** or 110, **111**, 112 Exodus 4.1–23 Hebrews 10.1–18	Psalms 52, **91** or 119.**129–152** Jeremiah 18.13–end John 10.11–21
Thursday 10 March — P(La)	Exodus 32.7–14 Psalm 106.19–23 John 5.31–end	Psalms 53, **86** or 113, **115** Exodus 4.27—6.1 Hebrews 10.19–25	Psalms **94** or 114, **116**, 117 Jeremiah 19.1–13 John 10.22–end
Friday 11 March — P(La)	Wisdom 2.1, 12–22 or Jeremiah 26.8–11 Psalm 34.15–end John 7.1–2, 10, 25–30	Psalm **102** or 139 Exodus 6.2–13 Hebrews 10.26–end	Psalms 13, **16** or **130**, 131, 137 Jeremiah 19.14—20.6 John 11.1–16
Saturday 12 March — P(La)	Jeremiah 11.18–20 Psalm 7.1–2, 8–10 John 7.40–52	Psalm **32** or 120, **121**, 122 Exodus 7.8–end Hebrews 11.1–16	Psalms **140**, 141, 142 or **118** Jeremiah 20.7–end John 11.17–27

		Principal Service	3rd Service	2nd Service
Sunday	13 March P(La) **5th Sunday of Lent** *Passiontide begins*	Isaiah 43.16–21 Psalm 126 Philippians 3.4b–14 John 12.1–8	Psalms 111, 112 Isaiah 35 Romans 7.21—8.4	Psalm 35 [or 35.1–9] 2 Chronicles 35.1–6, 10–16 Luke 22.1–13

The following readings may replace those provided for Holy Communion on any day during the Fifth Week of Lent (except the Festival of Joseph of Nazareth):
2 Kings 4.18–21, 32–37; Psalm 17.1–8, 16; John 11.1–45

		Holy Communion	Morning Prayer	Evening Prayer
Monday	14 March P(La)	Susannah 1–9, 15–17, 19–30, 33–62 [or 41b–62] or Joshua 2.1–14 Psalm 23 John 8.1–11	Psalms **73**, 121 or 123, 124, 125, **126** Exodus 8.1–19 Hebrews 11.17–31	Psalms **26**, 27 or **127**, 128, 129 Jeremiah 21.1–10 John 11.28–44
Tuesday	15 March P(La)	Numbers 21.4–9 Psalm 102.1–3, 16–23 John 8.21–30	Psalms **35**, 123 or **132**, 133 Exodus 8.20–end Hebrews 11.32—12.2	Psalms **61**, 64 or (134,) **135** Jeremiah 22.1–5, 13–19 John 11.45–end
Wednesday	16 March P(La)	Daniel 3.14–20, 24–25, 28 Canticle: Bless the Lord John 8.31–42	Psalms **55**, 124 or **119.153–end** Exodus 9.1–12 Hebrews 12.3–13	Psalms 56, **62** or **136** Jeremiah 22.20—23.8 John 12.1–11
Thursday	17 March P(L)w Patrick, bishop, missionary, patron of Ireland, c.460 (see p. 82)	Genesis 17.3–9 Psalm 105.4–9 John 8.51–end	Psalms **40**, 125 or **143**, 146 Exodus 9.13–end Hebrews 12.14–end	Psalms 42, **43** or **138**, 140, 141 Jeremiah 23.9–32 John 12.12–19
Friday	18 March P(La) Cyril, bishop, teacher of the faith, 386	Jeremiah 20.10–13 Psalm 18.1–6 John 10.31–end	Psalms **22**, 126 or 142, **144** Exodus 10 Hebrews 13.1–16	Psalm **31** or **145** Jeremiah 24 John 12.20–36a or: 1st EP of Joseph of Nazareth: Psalm 132; Hosea 11.1–9; Luke 2.41–end

		Principal Service	3rd Service	2nd Service
Saturday	19 March W Joseph of Nazareth	2 Samuel 7.4–16 Psalm 89.26–36 Romans 4.13–18 Matthew 1.18–end	MP Psalms 25, 147.1–12 Isaiah 11.1–10 Matthew 13.54–end	EP Psalms 1, 112 Genesis 50.22–end Matthew 2.13–end

Holy Week

		Principal Service	3rd Service	2nd Service
Sunday	**20 March** **Palm Sunday** — R	*Liturgy of the Palms:* Luke 19.28–40 Psalm 118.1–2,19–end [or 118.19–end] *Liturgy of the Passion:* Isaiah 50.4–9a Psalm 31.9–16 [or 31.9–18] Philippians 2.5–11 Luke 22.14—end of 23 or Luke 23.1–49	Psalms 61, 62 Zechariah 9.9–12 1 Corinthians 2.1–12	Psalm 69.1–20 Isaiah 5.1–7 Luke 20.9–19
		Holy Communion	**Morning Prayer**	**Evening Prayer**
			From the Monday of Holy Week until the Saturday of Easter Week the seasonal psalmody must be used.	
Monday	**21 March** Monday of Holy Week — R	Isaiah 42.1–9 Psalm 36.5–11 Hebrews 9.11–15 John 12.1–11	Psalm 41 Lamentations 1.1–12a Luke 22.1–23	Psalm 25 Lamentations 2.8–19 Colossians 1.18–23
Tuesday	**22 March** Tuesday of Holy Week — R	Isaiah 49.1–7 Psalm 71.1–14 [or 71.1–8] 1 Corinthians 1.18–31 John 12.20–36	Psalm 27 Lamentations 3.1–18 Luke 22. [24–38] 39–53	Psalm 55.13–24 Lamentations 3.40–51 Galatians 6.11–end
Wednesday	**23 March** Wednesday of Holy Week — R	Isaiah 50.4–9a Psalm 70 Hebrews 12.1–3 John 13.21–32	Psalm 102 [or 102.1–18] Wisdom 1.16—2.1; 2.12–22 or Jeremiah 11.18–20 Luke 22.54–end	Psalm 88 Isaiah 63.1–9 Revelation 14.18—15.4
Thursday	**24 March** Maundy Thursday — W	Exodus 12.1–4 [5–10] 11–14 Psalm 116.1, 10–end [or 116.9–end] 1 Corinthians 11.23–26 John 13.1–17, 31b–35	Psalms 42, 43 Leviticus 16.2–24 Luke 23.1–25	Psalm 39 Exodus 11 Ephesians 2.11–18
Friday	**25 March** Good Friday — Hangings removed; R for the Liturgy	Isaiah 52.13—end of 53 Psalm 22 [or 22.1–11 or 22.1–21] Hebrews 10.16–25 or Hebrews 4.14–16; 5.7–9 John 18.1—end of 19	Psalm 69 Genesis 22.1–18 A part of John 18 and 19 may be read, if not used at the Principal Service or Hebrews 10.1–10	Psalms 130, 143 Lamentations 5.15–end John 19.38–end or Colossians 1.18–23

		Principal Service	3rd Service	2nd Service
Saturday	**26 March** **Easter Eve** *Hangings removed* *These readings are for use at services other than the Easter Vigil.*	Job 14.1–14 or Lamentations 3.1–9, 19–24 Psalm 31.1–4, 15–16 [or 31.1–5] 1 Peter 4.1–8 Matthew 27.57–end or John 19.38–end	Psalm 142 Hosea 6.1–6 John 2.18–22	Psalm 116 Job 19.21–27 1 John 5.5–12
Saturday or Sunday	**26 March evening** **27 March morning** *Gold or W* *Easter Vigil* *The New Testament readings should be preceded by a minimum of three Old Testament readings.* *The Exodus reading should always be used.*	Genesis 1.1–2.4a Genesis 7.1–5, 11–18; 8.6–18; 9.8–13 Genesis 22.1–18 **Exodus 14.10–end; 15.20–21** Isaiah 55.1–11 Baruch 3.9–15, 32–4.4 or Proverbs 8.1–8, 19–21; 9.4b–6 Ezekiel 36.24–28 Ezekiel 37.1–14 Zephaniah 3.14–end **Romans 6.3–11** **Luke 24.1–12**	Psalm 136.1–9, 23–end Psalm 46 Psalm 16 **Canticle: Exodus 15.1b–13, 17–18** *Canticle:* Isaiah 12.2–end Psalm 19 Psalms 42, 43 Psalm 143 Psalm 98 **Psalm 114**	
Sunday	**27 March** **Easter Day** *Gold or W*	Acts 10.34–43† or Isaiah 65.17–end Psalm 118.1–2, 14–24 [or 118.14–24] 1 Corinthians 15.19–26 or Acts 10.34–43† John 20.1–18 or Luke 24.1–12 † *The reading from Acts must be used as either the first or second reading.*	*MP* Psalms 114, 117 Ezekiel 47.1–12 John 2.13–22	*EP* Psalms 105 or 66.1–11 Isaiah 43.1–21 1 Corinthians 15.1–11 or John 20.19–23

Easter Week

		Holy Communion	Morning Prayer	Evening Prayer
Monday	**28 March** W Monday of Easter Week	Acts 2.14, 22–32 Psalm 16.1–2, 6–end Matthew 28.8–15	Psalms 111, 117, 146 Exodus 12.1–14 1 Corinthians 15.1–11	Psalm **135** Song of Solomon 1.9—2.7 Mark 16.1–8
Tuesday	**29 March** W Tuesday of Easter Week	Acts 2.36–41 Psalm 33.4–5, 18–end John 20.11–18	Psalms **112**, 147.1–12 Exodus 12.14–36 1 Corinthians 15.12–19	Psalm **136** Song of Solomon 2.8–end Luke 24.1–12
Wednesday	**30 March** W Wednesday of Easter Week	Acts 3.1–10 Psalm 105.1–9 Luke 24.13–35	Psalms **113**, 147.13–end Exodus 12.37–end 1 Corinthians 15.20–28	Psalm **105** Song of Solomon 3 Matthew 28.16–end
Thursday	**31 March** W Thursday of Easter Week	Acts 3.11–end Psalm 8 Luke 24.35–48	Psalms **114**, 148 Exodus 13.1–16 1 Corinthians 15.29–34	Psalm **106** Song of Solomon 5.2—6.3 Luke 7.11–17
Friday	**1 April** W Friday of Easter Week	Acts 4.1–12 Psalm 118.1–4, 22–26 John 21.1–14	Psalms **115**, 149 Exodus 13.17—14.14 1 Corinthians 15.35–50	Psalm **107** Song of Solomon 7.10—8.4 Luke 8.41–end
Saturday	**2 April** W Saturday of Easter Week	Acts 4.13–21 Psalm 118.1–4, 14–21 Mark 16.9–15	Psalms **116**, 150 Exodus 14.15–end 1 Corinthians 15.51–end	Psalm **145** Song of Solomon 8.5–7 John 11.17–44

			Holy Communion	Morning Prayer	Evening Prayer
Sunday 3 April **2nd Sunday of Easter**		W	[Exodus 14.10–end; 15.20–21] Acts 5.27–32† Psalm 118.14–end or Psalm 150 Revelation 1.4–8 John 20.19–end † *The reading from Acts must be used as either the first or second reading.*	Psalm 136.1–16 Exodus 12.1–13 1 Peter 1.3–12	**1st EP of the Annunciation of Our Lord** Psalm 85 Wisdom 9.1–12 *or* Genesis 3.8–15 Galatians 4.1–5
Monday 4 April **Annunciation of Our Lord to the Blessed Virgin Mary** *(transferred from 25 March)*		*Gold or W*	Isaiah 7.10–14 Psalm 40.5–11 Hebrews 10.4–10 Luke 1.26–38	MP Psalms 111, 113 1 Samuel 2.1–10 Romans 5.12–end	EP Psalms 131, 146 Isaiah 52.1–12 Hebrews 2.5–end
Tuesday 5 April		W	Acts 4.32–end Psalm 93 John 3.7–15	Psalms **8**, 20, 21 or **5**, 6, (8) Exodus 15.22—16.10 Colossians 1.15–end	Psalm **104** or 9, **10*** Deuteronomy 1.19–40 John 20.11–18
Wednesday 6 April		W	Acts 5.17–26 Psalm 34.1–8 John 3.16–21	Psalms 16, **30** or 119.1–**32** Exodus 16.11–end Colossians 2.1–15	Psalm **33** or **11**, 12, 13 Deuteronomy 3.18–end John 20.19–end
Thursday 7 April		W	Acts 5.27–33 Psalm 34.1, 15–end John 3.31–end	Psalms **28**, 29 or 14, **15**, 16 Exodus 17 Colossians 2.16—3.11	Psalm **34** or **18*** Deuteronomy 4.1–14 John 21.1–14
Friday 8 April		W	Acts 5.34–42 Psalm 27.1–5, 16–17 John 6.1–15	Psalms 57, **61** or 17, **19** Exodus 18.1–12 Colossians 3.12—4.1	Psalm **118** or 22 Deuteronomy 4.15–31 John 21.15–19
Saturday 9 April *Dietrich Bonhoeffer, Lutheran pastor, martyr, 1945*		W	Acts 6.1–7 Psalm 33.1–5, 18–19 John 6.16–21	Psalms 63, **84** or 20, 21, **23** Exodus 18.13–end Colossians 4.2–end	Psalm **66** or **24**, 25 Deuteronomy 4.32–40 John 21.20–end

33

		Principal Service	3rd Service	2nd Service
Sunday	**10 April** W **3rd Sunday of Easter**	[Zephaniah 3.14–end] Acts 9.1–6 [7–20]† Psalm 30 Revelation 5.11–14 John 21.1–19 † *The reading from Acts must be used as either the first or second reading.*	Psalm 80.1–8 Exodus 15.1–2, 9–18 John 10.1–19	Psalm 86 Isaiah 38.9–20 John 11.[17–26] 27–44
		Holy Communion	**Morning Prayer**	**Evening Prayer**
Monday	**11 April** W *George Selwyn, bishop, 1878*	Acts 6.8–15 Psalm 119.17–24 John 6.22–29	Psalms **96**, 97 or 27, **30** Exodus 19 Luke 1.1–25	Psalms 61, 65 or 26, **28**, 29 Deuteronomy 5.1–22 Ephesians 1.1–14
Tuesday	**12 April** W	Acts 7.51—8.1a Psalm 31.1–5, 16 John 6.30–35	Psalms **98**, 99, 100 or 32, **36** Exodus 20.1–21 Luke 1.26–38	Psalm 71 or **33** Deuteronomy 5.22–end Ephesians 1.15–end
Wednesday	**13 April** W	Acts 8.1b–8 Psalm 66.1–6 John 6.35–40	Psalm 105 or **34** Exodus 24 Luke 1.39–56	Psalms 67, **72** or 119.**33–56** Deuteronomy 6 Ephesians 2.1–10
Thursday	**14 April** W	Acts 8.26–end Psalm 66.7–8, 14–end John 6.44–51	Psalm **136** or **37*** Exodus 25.1–22 Luke 1.57–end	Psalms **73** or 39, **40** Deuteronomy 7.1–11 Ephesians 2.11–end
Friday	**15 April** W	Acts 9.1–20 Psalm 117 John 6.52–59	Psalm 107 or **31** Exodus 28.1–4a, 29–38 Luke 2.1–20	Psalm 77 or **35** Deuteronomy 7.12–end Ephesians 3.1–13
Saturday	**16 April** W *Isabella Gilmore, deaconess, 1923*	Acts 9.31–42 Psalm 116.10–15 John 6.60–69	Psalms 108, **110**, 111 or 41, **42**, 43 Exodus 29.1–9 Luke 2.21–40	Psalms 23, **27** or 45, **46** Deuteronomy 8 Ephesians 3.14–end

Day	Date / Commemoration	Colour			
Sunday	**17 April** 4th Sunday of Easter	W	[Genesis 7.1–5, 11–18; 8.6–18; 9.8–13] Acts 9.36–end† Psalm 23 Revelation 7.9–end John 10.22–30 † The reading from Acts must be used as either the first or second reading.	Psalm 146 1 Kings 17.17–end Luke 7.11–23	Psalms 113, 114 Isaiah 63.7–14 Luke 24.36–49

			Holy Communion	**Morning Prayer**	**Evening Prayer**
Monday	**18 April**	W	Acts 11.1–18 Psalms 42.1–2, 43.1–4 John 10.1–10 (or 11–18)	Psalm 103 or 44 Exodus 32.1–14 Luke 2.41–end	Psalms 112, 113, **114** or **47**, 49 Deuteronomy 9.1–21 Ephesians 4.1–16
Tuesday	**19 April** Alphege, archbishop, martyr, 1012 (see p. 79)	Wr	Acts 11.19–26 Psalm 87 John 10.22–30	Psalm 139 or 48, 52 Exodus 32.15–34 Luke 3.1–14	Psalms 115, **116** or **50** Deuteronomy 9.23—10.5 Ephesians 4.17–end
Wednesday	**20 April**	W	Acts 12.24—13.5 Psalm 67 John 12.44–end	Psalm 135 or 119.57–80 Exodus 33 Luke 3.15–22	Psalms **47**, 48 or **59**, 60, (67) Deuteronomy 10.12–end Ephesians 5.1–14
Thursday	**21 April** Anselm, archbishop, teacher, 1109 (see p. 80)	W	Acts 13.13–25 Psalm 89.1–2, 20–26 John 13.16–20	Psalm 118 or 56, **57** (63*) Exodus 34.1–10, 27–end Luke 4.1–13	Psalms 81, **85** or 61, **62**, 64 Deuteronomy 11.8–end Ephesians 5.15–end
Friday	**22 April**	W	Acts 13.26–33 Psalm 2 John 14.1–6	Psalm 33 or **51**, 54 Exodus 35.20—36.7 Luke 4.14–30	Psalms 36, 40 or **38** Deuteronomy 12.1–14 Ephesians 6.1–9 or: 1st EP of George, martyr, patron of England: Psalms 111, 116; Jeremiah 15.15–end; Hebrews 11.32—12.2

			Principal Service	**3rd Service**	**2nd Service**
Saturday	**23 April** George, martyr, patron of England, c.304	R	1 Maccabees 2.59–64 or Revelation 12.7–12 Psalm 126 2 Timothy 2.3–13 John 15.18–21	MP Psalms 5, 146 Joshua 1.1–9 Ephesians 6.10–20	EP Psalms 3, 11 Isaiah 43.1–7 John 15.1–8

		Principal Service	3rd Service	2nd Service
Sunday **24 April** 5th Sunday of Easter	W	[Baruch 3.9–15, 32 —4.4 or Genesis 22.1–18] Acts 11.1–18† Psalm 148 [or 148.1–6] Revelation 21.1–6 John 13.31–35 † *The reading from Acts must be used as either the first or second reading.*	MP Psalms 37.23–end, 148 Isaiah 62.6–10 or Ecclesiasticus 51.13–end Acts 12.25—13.13	Psalm 98 Daniel 6. [1–5] 6–23 Mark 15.46—16.8 or: 1st EP of Mark the Evangelist: Psalm 19; Isaiah 52.7–10; Mark 1.1–15
Monday **25 April** Mark the Evangelist	R	Proverbs 15.28–end or Acts 15.35–end Psalm 119.9–16 Ephesians 4.7–16 Mark 13.5–13	Psalm 16 2 Samuel 7.4–13 Acts 2.14a, 22–32 [33–36]	EP Psalm 45 Ezekiel 1.4–14 2 Timothy 4.1–11
		Holy Communion	**Morning Prayer**	**Evening Prayer**
Tuesday **26 April**	W	Acts 14.19–end Psalm 145.10–end John 14.27–end	Psalms 19, 147.1–12 or **73** Numbers 11.1–33 Luke 5.1–11	Psalms 96, 97 or **74** Deuteronomy 17.8–end 1 Peter 1.13–end
Wednesday **27 April** *Christina Rossetti, poet, 1894*	W	Acts 15.1–6 Psalm 122.1–5 John 15.1–8	Psalms 30, 147.13–end or **77** Numbers 12 Luke 5.12–26	Psalms 98, **99**, 100 or **119.81–104** Deuteronomy 18.9–end 1 Peter 2.1–10
Thursday **28 April** *Peter Chanel, missionary, martyr 1841*	W	Acts 15.7–21 Psalm 96.1–3, 7–10 John 15.9–11	Psalms **57**, 148 or **78.1–39*** Numbers 13.1–3, 17–end Luke 5.27–end	Psalm **104** or **78.40–end*** Deuteronomy 19 1 Peter 2.11–end
Friday **29 April** *Catherine of Siena, teacher of the faith, 1380 (see p. 80)*	W	Acts 15.22–31 Psalm 57.8–end John 15.12–17	Psalms **138**, 149 or **55** Numbers 14.1–25 Luke 6.1–11	Psalm 66 or 69 Deuteronomy 21.22—22.8 1 Peter 3.1–12
Saturday **30 April** *Pandita Mary Ramabai, translator, 1922*	W	Acts 16.1–10 Psalm 100 John 15.18–21	Psalms **146**, 150 or **76**, 79 Numbers 14.26–end Luke 6.12–26	Psalm 118 or 81, **84** Deuteronomy 24.5–end 1 Peter 3.13–end

	Principal Service	Third Service	Second Service
Sunday 1 May W **6th Sunday of Easter**	[Ezekiel 37.1–14] Acts 16.9–15† Psalm 67 Revelation 21.10, 22—22.5 John 14.23–29 or John 5.1–9 † *The reading from Acts must be used as either the first or second reading.*	Psalm 40.1–9 Genesis 1.26–28 [29–end] Colossians 3.1–11	Psalms 126, 127 Zephaniah 3.14–end Matthew 28.1–10, 16–end or: 1st EP of Philip and James, Apostles: Psalm 25; Isaiah 40.27–end; John 12.20–26
Monday 2 May R Philip and James, Apostles *(transferred from 1 May)* Rogation Day	Isaiah 30.15–21 Psalm 119.1–8 Ephesians 1.3–10 John 14.1–14	MP Psalms 139, 146 Proverbs 4.10–18 James 1.1–12	EP Psalm 149 Job 23.1–12 John 1.43–end

	Holy Communion	Morning Prayer	Evening Prayer
Tuesday 3 May W Rogation Day	Acts 16.22–34 Psalm 138 John 16.5–11	Psalms 124, 125, **126**, 127 or 87, **89.1–18** Numbers 16.36–end Luke 6.39–end	Psalms **128**, 129, 130, 131 or **89.19–end** Deuteronomy 28.1–14 1 Peter 4.12–end
Wednesday 4 May W Rogation Day English Saints and Martyrs of the Reformation Era	Acts 17.15, 22—18.1 Psalm 148.1–2, 11–end John 16.12–15 *Lesser Festival Eucharistic lectionary:* Isaiah 43.1–7 or Ecclesiasticus 2.10–17; Psalm 87; 2 Corinthians 4.5–12; John 12.20–26	Psalms **132**, 133 or **119.105–128** Numbers 17.1–11 Luke 7.1–10	**1st EP of Ascension Day:** Psalms 15, 24 2 Samuel 23.1–5 Colossians 2.20—3.4

37

Ascension Day

		Principal Service	3rd Service	2nd Service
Thursday	**5 May** W	Acts 1.1–11† or Daniel 7.9–14	MP Psalms 110, 150	EP Psalm 8
	Ascension Day	Psalm 47 or Psalm 93	Isaiah 52.7–end	Song of the Three 29–37
		Ephesians 1.15–end or Acts 1.1–11†	Hebrews 7. [11–25] 26–end	or 2 Kings 2.1–15
		Luke 24.44–end		Revelation 5
		† The reading from Acts must be used		HC Matthew 28.16–end
		as either the first or second reading.		

The nine days after Ascension Day until the eve of Pentecost are observed as days of prayer and preparation for the celebration of the outpouring of the Holy Spirit.

From 6 to 14 May, in preparation for the Day of Pentecost, an alternative sequence of daily readings for use at the one of the offices is marked with an asterisk.*

		Holy Communion	Morning Prayer	Evening Prayer
Friday	**6 May** W	Acts 18.9–18	Psalms 20, **81** or **88**, (95)	Psalm **145** or **102**
		Psalm 47.1–6	Numbers 20.1–13	Deuteronomy 29.2–15
		John 16.20–23	Luke 7.11–17	1 John 1.1—2.6
			Exodus 35.30—36.1; Galatians 5.13–end	
Saturday	**7 May** W	Acts 18.22–end	Psalms 21, **47** or 96, **97**, 100	Psalms 84, **85** or **104**
		Psalm 47.1–2, 7–end	Numbers 21.4–9	Deuteronomy 30
		John 16.23–28	Luke 7.18–35	1 John 2.7–17
			Numbers 11.16–17, 24–29; 1 Corinthians 2	

		Holy Communion	Morning Prayer	Evening Prayer
Sunday 8 May **7th Sunday of Easter** *Sunday after Ascension Day*	W	[Ezekiel 36.24–28] Acts 16.16–34† Psalm 97 Revelation 22.12–14, 16–17, 20–end John 17.20–end † *The reading from Acts must be used as either the first or second reading.*	Psalm 99 Deuteronomy 34 Luke 24.44–end or Acts 1.1–8	Psalm 68 [or 68.1–3, 18–19] Isaiah 44.1–8 Ephesians 4.7–16 HC Luke 24.44–end
Monday 9 May	W	Acts 19.1–8 Psalm 68.1–6 John 16.29–end	Psalms 93, 96, 97 or **98**, 99, 101 Numbers 22.1–35 Luke 7.36–end *Numbers 27.15–end; 1 Corinthians 3*	Psalm **18** or 105* (or 103) Deuteronomy 31.1–13 1 John 2.18–end
Tuesday 10 May	W	Acts 20.17–27 Psalm 68.9–10, 18–19 John 17.1–11	Psalms 98, **99**, 100 or **106*** (or 103) Numbers 22.36—23.12 Luke 8.1–15 *1 Samuel 10.1–10; 1 Corinthians 12.1–13*	Psalm **68** or 107* Deuteronomy 31.14–29 1 John 3.1–10
Wednesday 11 May	W	Acts 20.28–end Psalm 68.27–28, 32–end John 17.11–19	Psalms 2, **29** or 110, **111**, 112 Numbers 23.13–end Luke 8.16–25 *1 Kings 19.1–18; Matthew 3.13–end*	Psalms 36, **46** or 119.**129–152** Deuteronomy 31.30—32.14 1 John 3.11–end
Thursday 12 May	W	Acts 22.30, 23.6–11 Psalm 16.1, 5–end John 17.20–end	Psalms **24**, 72 or 113, **115** Numbers 24 Luke 8.26–39 *Ezekiel 11.14–20; Matthew 9.35—10.20*	Psalm 139 or 114, **116**, 117 Deuteronomy 32.15–47 1 John 4.1–6
Friday 13 May	W	Acts 25.13–21 Psalm 103.1–2, 11–12, 19–20 John 21.15–19	Psalms **28**, 30 or **139** Numbers 27.12–end Luke 8.40–end *Ezekiel 36.22–28; Matthew 12.22–32*	Psalm 147 or **130**, 131, 137 Deuteronomy 33 1 John 4.7–end *or:* 1st EP of Matthias the Apostle: Psalm 147.1; Isaiah 22.15–22; Philippians 3.13b—4.1

		Principal Service	3rd Service	2nd Service
Saturday 14 May Matthias the Apostle	R	Isaiah 22.15–end or Acts 1.15–end Psalm 15 Acts 1.15–end or 1 Corinthians 4.1–7 John 15.9–17	MP Psalms 16, 147.1–12 1 Samuel 2.27–35 Acts 2.37–end	**1st EP of Pentecost:** Psalm 48 Deuteronomy 16.9–15 John 7.37–39

Pentecost / Ordinary Time

		Principal Service	3rd Service	2nd Service
Sunday	**15 May** **Pentecost** *Whit Sunday*	Acts 2.1–21† or Genesis 11.1–9 Psalm 104.26–36,37b [or 104.26–end] Romans 8.14–17 or Acts 2.1–21† John 14.8–17 [25–27] † *The reading from Acts must be used as either the first or second reading.*	MP Psalms 36.5–10; 150 Isaiah 40.12–23 or Wisdom 9.9–17 1 Corinthians 2.6–end	EP Psalm 33.1–12 Exodus 33.7–20 2 Corinthians 3.4–end HC John 16.4b–15
	R			
		Holy Communion	Morning Prayer	Evening Prayer
Monday	**16 May** Ordinary Time resumes today. *Caroline Chisholm, Social Reformer, 1877.* DEL week 7	James 3.13–end Psalm 19.7–end Mark 9.14–29	Psalms 123, 124, 125, **126** Joshua 1 Luke 9.18–27	Psalms **127**, 128, 129 Job 1 Romans 1.1–17
	G			
Tuesday	**17 May**	James 4.1–10 Psalm 55.7–9, 24 Mark 9.30–37	Psalms **132**, 133 Joshua 2 Luke 9.28–36	Psalms (134) **135** Job 2 Romans 1.18–end
	G			
Wednesday	**18 May**	James 4.13–end Psalm 49.1–2, 5–10 Mark 9.38–40	Psalm **119.153–end** Joshua 3 Luke 9.37–50	Psalm **136** Job 3 Romans 2.1–16
	G			
Thursday	**19 May** *Dunstan, archbishop, monastic reformer, 988 (see p. 81)*	James 5.1–6 Psalm 49.12–20 Mark 9.41–50	Psalms **143**, 146 Joshua 4.1—5.1 Luke 9.51–end	Psalms **138**, 140, 141 Job 4 Romans 2.17–end
	Gw			
Friday	**20 May** *Alcuin, deacon, abbot, 804 (see p. 82)*	James 5.9–12 Psalm 103.1–4, 8–13 Mark 10.1–12	Psalms 142, **144** Joshua 5.2–end Luke 10.1–16	Psalm **45** Job 5 Romans 3.1–20
	Gw			
Saturday	**21 May** *Helena, protector of the Holy Places, 330*	James 5.13–end Psalm 141.1–4 Mark 10.13–16	Psalm **147** Joshua 6.1–20 Luke 10.17–24	**1st EP of Trinity Sunday:** Psalms 97, 98 Isaiah 40.12–end Mark 1.1–13
	G			

Sunday

22 May Trinity Sunday — *Gold or W*

	3rd Service	2nd Service
Principal Service Proverbs 8.1–4, 22–31 Psalm 8 Romans 5.1–5 John 16.12–15	MP Psalm 29 Isaiah 6.1–8 Revelation 4	EP Psalm 73.1–3, 16–end Exodus 3.1–15 John 3.1–17

Monday

23 May — *G*
DEL week 8

Holy Communion	Morning Prayer	Evening Prayer
1 Peter 1.3–9 Psalm 111 Mark 10.17–27	Psalms 1, 2, 3 Joshua 7.1–15 Luke 10.25–37	Psalms **4**, 7 Job 7 Romans 4.1–12

Tuesday

24 May — *Gw*
John and Charles Wesley, evangelists,
hymn writers, 1791 and 1788 (see p. 81)

Holy Communion	Morning Prayer	Evening Prayer
1 Peter 1.10–16 Psalm 98.1–5 Mark 10.28–31	Psalms **5**, 6 (8) Joshua 7.16–end Luke 10.38–end	Psalms **9**, 10* Job 8 Romans 4.13–end

Wednesday

25 May — *Gw*
The Venerable Bede, monk, scholar,
historian, 735 (see p. 82)
Aldhelm, bishop, 709

Holy Communion	Morning Prayer	Evening Prayer
1 Peter 1.18–end Psalm 147.13–end Mark 10.32–45	Psalm **119.1–32** Joshua 8.1–29 Luke 11.1–13	Psalms **11**, 12, 13 Job 9 Romans 5.1–11

or: 1st EP of Corpus Christi: Psalms 110, 111; Exodus 16.2–15; John 6.22–35

Thursday

26 May — *W*
Day of Thanksgiving for the Institution
of the Holy Communion (Corpus Christi)

Principal Service	3rd Service	2nd Service
Genesis 14.18–20 Psalm 116.10–end 1 Corinthians 11.23–26 John 6.51–58	MP Psalm 147 Deuteronomy 8.2–16 1 Corinthians 10.1–17	EP Psalms 23, 42, 43 Proverbs 9.1–5 Luke 9.11–17

Alternatively Corpus Christi may be kept as a Lesser Festival, and either these readings or those given below may be used.

or Thursday

26 May — *Gw*
Day of Thanksgiving for the Institution
of the Holy Communion (Corpus Christi)
Augustine, archbishop, 605 (see p. 81)
John Calvin, reformer, 1564
Philip Neri, founder of the Oratorians,
spiritual guide, 1595

Holy Communion	Morning Prayer	Evening Prayer
1 Peter 2.2–5, 9–12 Psalm 100 Mark 10.46–end	Psalms 14, **15**, 16 Joshua 8.30–end Luke 11.14–28	Psalm **18*** Job 10 Romans 5.12–end

Friday

27 May — *G*

Holy Communion	Morning Prayer	Evening Prayer
1 Peter 4.7–13 Psalm 96.10–end Mark 11.11–26	Psalms 17, **19** Joshua 9.3–26 Luke 11.29–36	Psalm **22** Job 11 Romans 6.1–14

Saturday

28 May — *G*
Lanfranc, monk, archbishop, scholar, 1089

Holy Communion	Morning Prayer	Evening Prayer
Jude 17, 20–end Psalm 63.1–6 Mark 11.27–end	Psalms 20, 21, **23** Joshua 10.1–15 Luke 11.37–end	Psalms **24**, 25 Job 12 Romans 6.15–end

Trinity 1

	Principal Service	3rd Service	2nd Service
Sunday **29 May** G **1st Sunday after Trinity** Proper 4	*Continuous:* 1 Kings 18.20–21 [22–29] 30–39 Psalm 96 *Related:* 1 Kings 8.22–23, 41–43 Psalm 96.1–9 Galatians 1.1–12 Luke 7.1–10	Psalm 41 Deuteronomy 5.1–21 Acts 21.17–39a	Psalm 39 Genesis 4.1–16 Mark 3.7–19

	Holy Communion	Morning Prayer	Evening Prayer
Monday **30 May** Gw *Josephine Butler, Social Reformer, 1906 (see p.83)* *Joan of Arc, visionary, 1431* *Apolo Kivebulaya, priest, evangelist, 1933* DEL week 9	2 Peter 1.2–7 Psalm 91.1–2, 14–end Mark 12.1–12	Psalms 27, **30** Joshua 14 Luke 12.1–12	Psalms 26, **28**, 29 Job 13 Romans 7.1–6 *or: 1st EP of the Visit of the BVM to Elizabeth:* Psalm 45; Song of Solomon 2.8–14; Luke 1.26–38

	Principal Service	3rd Service	2nd Service
Tuesday **31 May** W Visit of the Blessed Virgin Mary to Elizabeth	Zephaniah 3.14–18 Psalm 113 Romans 12.9–16 Luke 1.39–49 [50–56]	MP Psalms 85, 150 1 Samuel 2.1–10 Mark 3.31–end	EP Psalms 122, 127, 128 Zechariah 2.10–end John 3.25–30

	Holy Communion	Morning Prayer	Evening Prayer
Wednesday **1 June** Gr *Justin, martyr, c.165 (see p.79)*	2 Timothy 1.1–3, 6–12 Psalm 123 Mark 12.18–27	Psalm **34** Joshua 22.9–end Luke 12.22–31	Psalm 119.**33**–56 Job 15 Romans 8.1–11
Thursday **2 June** G	2 Timothy 2.8–15 Psalm 25.4–12 Mark 12.28–34	Psalm **37*** Joshua 23 Luke 12.32–40	Psalms 39, **40** Job 16.1–17.2 Romans 8.12–17
Friday **3 June** G *Martyrs of Uganda, 1885–7, 1977*	2 Timothy 3.10–end Psalm 119.161–168 Mark 12.35–37	Psalm **31** Joshua 24.1–28 Luke 12.41–48	Psalm **35** Job 17.3–end Romans 8.18–30
Saturday **4 June** G *Petroc, abbot, 6th cent*	2 Timothy 4.1–8 Psalm 71.7–16 Mark 12.38–end	Psalms 41, **42**, 43 Joshua 24.29–end Luke 12.49–end	Psalms 45, **46** Job 18 Romans 8.31–end

		Principal Service			3rd Service	2nd Service

		Principal Service			**3rd Service**	**2nd Service**
Sunday	**5 June** G **2nd Sunday after Trinity** Proper 5	*Continuous:* 1 Kings 17.8–16 [17–end] Psalm 146	*Related:* 1 Kings 17.17–end Psalm 30 Galatians 1.11–end Luke 7.11–17		Psalm 45 Deuteronomy 6.10–end Acts 22.22—23.11	Psalm **44** [or 44.1–9] Genesis 8.15—9.17 Mark 4.1–20

		Holy Communion			**Morning Prayer**	**Evening Prayer**
Monday	**6 June** G Ini Kopuria, founder of the Melanesian Brotherhood, 1945 DEL week 10	1 Kings 17.1–6 Psalm 121 Matthew 5.1–12			Psalm **44** Judges 2 Luke 13.1–9	Psalms **47**, 49 Job 1 Romans 9.1–18
Tuesday	**7 June** G	1 Kings 17.7–16 Psalm 4 Matthew 5.13–16			Psalms **48**, 52 Judges 4.1–23 Luke 13.10–21	Psalm **50** Job 21 Romans 9.19–end
Wednesday	**8 June** Gw Thomas Ken, bishop, nonjuror, hymn writer, 1711 (see p.81)	1 Kings 18.20–39 Psalm 16.1, 6–end Matthew 5.17–19			Psalm **119.57–80** Judges 5 Luke 13.22–end	Psalms **59**, 60 (67) Job 22 Romans 10.1–10
Thursday	**9 June** Gw Columba, abbot, missionary, 597 (see p.82) Ephrem, deacon, hymn writer, teacher of the faith, 373	1 Kings 18.41–end Psalm 65.8–end Matthew 5.20–26			Psalms 56, **57** (63*) Judges 6.1–24 Luke 14.1–11	Psalms 61, **62**, 64 Job 23 Romans 10.11–end
Friday	**10 June** G	1 Kings 19.9, 11–16 Psalm 27.8–16 Matthew 5.27–32			Psalms **51**, 54 Judges 6.25–end Luke 14.12–24	Psalm **38** Job 24 Romans 11.1–12 *or:* 1st EP of Barnabas the Apostle: Psalms 1, 15; Isaiah 42.5–12; Acts 14.8–end

		Principal Service			**3rd Service**	**2nd Service**
Saturday	**11 June** R Barnabas the Apostle	Job 29.11–16 or Acts 11.19–end Psalm 112 Acts 11.19–end or Galatians 2.1–10 John 15.12–17			MP Psalms 100, 101, 117 Jeremiah 9.23–24 Acts 4.32–end	EP Psalm 147 Ecclesiastes 12.9–end or Tobit 4.5–11 Acts 9.26–31

43

Trinity 3

		Principal Service	3rd Service	2nd Service
Sunday **12 June** **3rd Sunday after Trinity** Proper 6	G	Continuous: 1 Kings 21.1–10 [11–14] 15–21a Psalm 5.1–8 *Related:* 2 Samuel 11.26—12.10, 13–15 Psalm 32 Galatians 2.15–end Luke 7.36 – 8.3	Psalm 49 Deuteronomy 10.12—11.1 Acts 23.12–end	Psalm 52 [53] Genesis 13 Mark 4.21–end
		Holy Communion	**Morning Prayer**	**Evening Prayer**
Monday **13 June** DEL week 11	G	1 Kings 21.1–16 Psalm 5.1–5 Matthew 5.38–42	Psalm 71 Judges 8.22–end Luke 15.1–10	Psalms 72, 75 Job 27 Romans 11.25–end
Tuesday **14 June** *Richard Baxter, puritan divine, 1691*	G	1 Kings 21.17–end Psalm 5.1–9 Matthew 5.43–end	Psalm 73 Judges 9.1–21 Luke 15.11–end	Psalm 74 Job 28 Romans 12.1–8
Wednesday **15 June** *Evelyn Underhill, spiritual writer, 1941*	G	2 Kings 2.1, 6–14 Psalm 31.21–end Matthew 6.1–6, 16–18	Psalm 77 Judges 9.22–end Luke 16.1–18	Psalm 119.81–104 Job 29 Romans 12.9–end
Thursday **16 June** *Richard, bishop, 1253 (see p. 81)* *Joseph Butler, bishop, philosopher, 1752*	Gw	Ecclesiasticus 48.1–14 or Isaiah 63.7–9 Psalm 97.1–8 Matthew 6.7–15	Psalm 78.1–39* Judges 11.1–11 Luke 16.19–end	Psalm 78.40–end* Job 30 Romans 13.1–7
Friday **17 June** *Samuel and Henrietta Barnett, social reformers, 1913 and 1936*	G	2 Kings 11.1–4, 9–18, 20 Psalm 132.1–5, 11–13 Matthew 6.19–23	Psalm 55 Judges 11.29–end Luke 17.1–10	Psalm 69 Job 31 Romans 13.8–end
Saturday **18 June** *Bernard Mizeki, martyr, 1896*	G	2 Chronicles 24.17–25 Psalm 89.25–33 Matthew 6.24–end	Psalms 76, 79 Judges 12.1–7 Luke 17.11–19	Psalms 81, 84 Job 32 Romans 14.1–12

		3rd Service / Morning Prayer	2nd Service / Evening Prayer
Sunday 19 June 4th Sunday after Trinity Proper 7	G	*Continuous:* 1 Kings 19.1–4 [5–7] 8–15a Psalms 42, 43 [or 42 or 43] *Related:* Isaiah 65.1–9 Psalm 22.19–28 Galatians 3.23–end Luke 8.26–39 Psalm 55.1–16, 18–21 Deuteronomy 11.1–15 Acts 27.1–12	**Evening Prayer** Psalms [50] 57 Genesis 24.1–27 Mark 5.21–end

Holy Communion

		Holy Communion	Morning Prayer	Evening Prayer
Monday 20 June DEL week 12	G	2 Kings 17.5–8, 13–15, 18 Psalm 60.1–5, 11–end Matthew 7.1–5	Psalms 80, 82 Judges 13.1–24 Luke 17.20–end	Psalms 85, 86 Job 33 Romans 14.13–end
Tuesday 21 June	G	2 Kings 19.9b–11, 14–21, 31–36 Psalm 48.1–2, 8–end Matthew 7.6, 12–14	Psalms 87, **89.1–18** Judges 14 Luke 18.1–14	Psalm **89.19–end** Job 38 Romans 15.1–13
Wednesday 22 June Alban, first martyr of Britain, c.250 (see p. 79) Ember Day	Gr	2 Kings 22.8–13, 23.1–3 Psalm 119.33–40 Matthew 7.15–20	Psalm **119.105–128** Judges 15.1—16.3 Luke 18.15–30	Psalms **91**, 93 Job 39 Romans 15.14–21
Thursday 23 June Etheldreda, abbess, c.678 (see p. 82)	Gw	2 Kings 24.8–17 Psalm 79.1–9, 12 Matthew 7.21–end	Psalms 90, **92** Judges 16.4–end Luke 18.31–end	Psalm **94** Job 40 Romans 15.22–end *or:* 1st EP of the Birth of John the Baptist: Psalm 71; Judges 13.2–7, 24–end; Luke 1.5–25

		Principal Service	3rd Service	2nd Service
Friday 24 June Birth of John the Baptist Ember Day	W	Isaiah 40.1–11 Psalm 85.7–end Acts 13.14b–26 or Galatians 3.23–end Luke 1.57–66, 80	*MP* Psalms 50, 149 Ecclesiasticus 48.1–10 or Malachi 3.1–6 Luke 3.1–17	*EP* Psalms 80, 82 Malachi 4 Matthew 11.2–19

		Holy Communion	Morning Prayer	Evening Prayer
Saturday 25 June Ember Day	G	Lamentations 2.2, 10–14, 18–19 Psalm 74.1–3, 21–end Matthew 8.5–17	Psalms 96, **97**, 100 Judges 18.1–20, 27–end Luke 19.1–27	Psalm **104** Job 42 Romans 16.17–end

Trinity 5

		Principal Service	3rd Service	2nd Service
Sunday	**26 June** **5th Sunday after Trinity** Proper 8 — G	Continuous: 2 Kings 2.1–2, 6–14 Psalm 77.1–2, 11–end [or 77.1–end] *Related:* 1 Kings 19.15–16, 19–end Psalm 16 Galatians 5.1, 13–25 Luke 9.51–end	Psalm 64 Deuteronomy 15.1–11 Acts 27.[13–32] 33–end	Psalms [59.1–6, 18–end] 60 Genesis 27.1–40 Mark 6.1–6

		Holy Communion	Morning Prayer	Evening Prayer
Monday	**27 June** *Cyril, bishop, teacher of the faith, 444* DEL week 13 — G	Amos 2.6–10, 13–end Psalm 50.16–23 Matthew 8.18–22	Psalms 98, 99, 101 1 Samuel 1.1–20 Luke 19.28–40	Psalm 105* (or 103) Ezekiel 1.1–14 2 Corinthians 1.1–14
Tuesday	**28 June** *Irenaeus, bishop, teacher of the faith, c.200 (see p.80)* — Gw	Amos 3.1–8; 4.11–12 Psalm 5.8–end Matthew 8.23–27	Psalm 106* (or 103) 1 Samuel 1.21—2.11 Luke 19.41–end	Psalm 107* Ezekiel 1.15—2.2 2 Corinthians 1.15—2.4 or: 1st EP of Peter and Paul, Apostles [or †Peter the Apostle alone]: Psalms 66, 67; Ezekiel 3.4–11; Galatians 1.13—2.8 [†Acts 9.32–end]

		Principal Service	3rd Service	2nd Service
Wednesday	**29 June** Peter and Paul, Apostles — R or Peter the Apostle — R	*Peter and Paul:* Zechariah 4.1–6a, 10b–end or Acts 12.1–11 Psalm 125 Acts 12.1–11 or 2 Timothy 4.6–8, 17–18 Matthew 16.13–19 *Peter alone:* Ezekiel 3.22–end or Acts 12.1–11 Psalm 125 Acts 12.1–11 or 1 Peter 2.19–end Matthew 16.13–19	MP Psalms 71, 113 Isaiah 49.1–6 Acts 11.1–18	EP Psalms 124, 138 Ezekiel 34.11–16 John 21.15–22

		Holy Communion	Morning Prayer	Evening Prayer
Thursday	**30 June** — G	Amos 7.10–end Psalm 19.7–10 Matthew 9.1–8	Psalms 113, 115 1 Samuel 2.27–end Luke 20.9–19	Psalms 114, 116, 117 Ezekiel 3.12–end 2 Corinthians 3
Friday	**1 July** *Henry, John and Henry Venn, priests, evangelical divines, 1797, 1813, 1873* — G	Amos 8.4–6, 9–12 Psalm 119.1–8 Matthew 9.9–13	Psalm 139 1 Samuel 3.1—4.1a Luke 20.20–26	Psalms 130, 131, 137 Ezekiel 8 2 Corinthians 4
Saturday	**2 July** — G	Amos 9.11–end Psalm 85.8–end Matthew 9.14–17	Psalms 120, 121, 122 1 Samuel 4.1b–end Luke 20.27–40	Psalm 118 Ezekiel 9 2 Corinthians 5

		Principal Service	3rd Service	2nd Service
Sunday 3 July Thomas the Apostle	R	Habakkuk 2.1–4 Psalm 31.1–6 Ephesians 2.19–end John 20.24–29	MP Psalms 92, 146 2 Samuel 15.17–21 or Ecclesiasticus 2 John 11.1–16	EP Psalm 139 Job 42.1–6 1 Peter 1.3–12
		Holy Communion	**Morning Prayer**	**Evening Prayer**
Monday 4 July DEL week 14	G	Hosea 2.14–16, 19–20 Psalm 145.2–9 Matthew 9.18–26	Psalms 123, 124, 125, **126** 1 Samuel 5 Luke 20.41—21.4	Psalms **127**, 128, 129 Ezekiel 10.1–19 2 Corinthians 6.1—7.1

If Thomas the Apostle is transferred to Monday 4 July:

		Principal Service	3rd Service	2nd Service
Sunday 3 July **6th Sunday after Trinity** Proper 9	G	*Continuous:* 2 Kings 5.1–14 Psalm 30 *Related:* Isaiah 66.10–14 Psalm 66.1–8 Galatians 6.[1–6] 7–16 Luke 10.1–11, 16–20	Psalm 74 Deuteronomy 24.10–end Acts 28.1–16	Psalms 65 [70] Genesis 29.1–20 Mark 6.7–29 *or:* 1st EP of Thomas the Apostle: Psalm 27; Isaiah 35; Hebrews 10.35—11.1
Monday 4 July Thomas the Apostle	R	Habakkuk 2.1–4 Psalm 31.1–6 Ephesians 2.19–end John 20.24–29	MP Psalms 92, 146 2 Samuel 15.17–21 or Ecclesiasticus 2 John 11.1–16	EP Psalm 139 Job 42.1–6 1 Peter 1.3–12

Trinity 6

		Holy Communion	Morning Prayer	Evening Prayer
Tuesday **5 July** DEL week 14	G	Hosea 8.4–7, 11–13 Psalm 103.8–12 Matthew 9.32–end	Psalms **132**, 133 1 Samuel 6.1–16 Luke 21.5–19	Psalms (134), **135** Ezekiel 11.14–end 2 Corinthians 7.2–end
Wednesday **6 July** *Thomas More, scholar, and John Fisher, bishop, martyrs, 1535*	G	Hosea 10.1–3, 7–8, 12 Psalm 115.3–10 Matthew 10.1–7	Psalm 119.**153–end** 1 Samuel 7 Luke 21.20–28	Psalm **136** Ezekiel 12.1–16 2 Corinthians 8.1–15
Thursday **7 July**	G	Hosea 11.1, 3–4, 8–9 Psalm 105.1–7 Matthew 10.7–15	Psalms **143**, 146 1 Samuel 8 Luke 21.29–end	Psalms **138**, 140, 141 Ezekiel 12.17–end 2 Corinthians 8.16—9.5
Friday **8 July**	G	Hosea 14.2–end Psalm 80.1–7 Matthew 10.16–23	Psalms 142, **144** 1 Samuel 9.1–14 Luke 22.1–13	Psalm **145** Ezekiel 13.1–16 2 Corinthians 9.6–end
Saturday **9 July**	G	Isaiah 6.1–8 Psalm 51.1–7 Matthew 10.24–33	Psalm **147** 1 Samuel 9.15—10.1 Luke 22.14–23	Psalms **148**, 149, 150 Ezekiel 14.1–11 2 Corinthians 10

		Holy Communion		Morning Prayer	Evening Prayer

Sunday — 10 July, 7th Sunday after Trinity, Proper 10 — G

Continuous: Amos 7.7–end, Psalm 82
Related: Deuteronomy 30.9–14, Psalm 25.1–10
Colossians 1.1–14
Luke 10.25–37

Psalm 76, Deuteronomy 28.1–14, Acts 28.17–end

Psalm 77 [or 77.1–12], Genesis 32.9–30, Mark 7.1–23

Monday — 11 July, Benedict, abbot, c.550 (see p.82), DEL week 15 — Gw

Holy Communion: Isaiah 1.11–17, Psalm 50.7–15, Matthew 10.34—11.1
Morning Prayer: Psalms 1, 2, 3, 1 Samuel 10.1–16, Luke 22.24–30
Evening Prayer: Psalms 4, 7, Ezekiel 14.12–end, 2 Corinthians 11.1–15

Tuesday — 12 July — G

Holy Communion: Isaiah 7.1–9, Psalm 48.1–7, Matthew 11.20–24
Morning Prayer: Psalms 5, 6 (8), 1 Samuel 10.17–end, Luke 22.31–38
Evening Prayer: Psalms 9, 10*, Ezekiel 18.1–20, 2 Corinthians 11.16–end

Wednesday — 13 July — G

Holy Communion: Isaiah 10.5–7, 13–16, Psalm 94.5–11, Matthew 11.25–27
Morning Prayer: Psalm 119.1–32, 1 Samuel 11, Luke 22.39–46
Evening Prayer: Psalms 11, 12, 13, Ezekiel 18.21–32, 2 Corinthians 12

Thursday — 14 July, John Keble, priest, poet, 1866 (see p.81) — Gw

Holy Communion: Isaiah 26.7–9, 16–19, Psalm 102.14–21, Matthew 11.28–end
Morning Prayer: Psalms 14, 15, 16, 1 Samuel 12, Luke 22.47–62
Evening Prayer: Psalm 18*, Ezekiel 20.1–20, 2 Corinthians 13

Friday — 15 July, Swithun, bishop, c.862 (see p.81), Bonaventure, friar, bishop, teacher of the faith, 1274 — Gw

Holy Communion: Isaiah 38.1–6, 21–22, 7–8 [sic], Canticle: Isaiah 38.10–16 or Psalm 32.1–8, Matthew 12.1–8
Morning Prayer: Psalms 17, 19, 1 Samuel 13.5–18, Luke 22.63–end
Evening Prayer: Psalm 22, Ezekiel 20.21–38, James 1.1–11

Saturday — 16 July, Osmund, bishop, 1099 — G

Holy Communion: Micah 2.1–5, Psalm 10.1–5a, 12, Matthew 12.14–21
Morning Prayer: Psalms 20, 21, 23, 1 Samuel 13.19—14.15, Luke 23.1–12
Evening Prayer: Psalms 24, 25, Ezekiel 24.15–end, James 1.12–end

Trinity 8

		Principal Service	3rd Service	2nd Service
Sunday 17 July **8th Sunday after Trinity** Proper 11	G	*Continuous:* Amos 8.1–12 Psalm 52 *Related:* Genesis 18.1–10a Psalm 15 Colossians 1.15–28 Luke 10.38–end	Psalms 82, 100 Deuteronomy 30.1–10 1 Peter 3.8–18	Psalm 81 Genesis 41.1–16, 25–37 1 Corinthians 4.8–13 HC John 4.31–35
		Holy Communion	**Morning Prayer**	**Evening Prayer**
Monday 18 July *Elizabeth Ferard, deaconess, founder of the Community of St Andrew, 1883* DEL week 16	G	Micah 6.1–4, 6–8 Psalm 50.3–7, 14 Matthew 12.38–42	Psalms 27, **30** 1 Samuel 14.24–46 Luke 23.13–25	Psalms 26, **28**, 29 Ezekiel 28.1–19 James 2.1–13
Tuesday 19 July *Gregory, bishop, and his sister Macrina, deaconess, teachers of the faith, c.394 and c.379 (see p. 80)*	Gw	Micah 7.14–15, 18–20 Psalm 85.1–7 Matthew 12.46–end	Psalms 32, **36** 1 Samuel 15.1–23 Luke 23.26–43	Psalm 33 Ezekiel 33.1–20 James 2.14–end
Wednesday 20 July *Margaret of Antioch, martyr, 4th cent Bartolomé de las Casas, Apostle to the Indies, 1566*	G	Jeremiah 1.1, 4–10 Psalm 70 Matthew 13.1–9	Psalm **34** 1 Samuel 16 Luke 23.44–56a	Psalm 119.33–**56** Ezekiel 33.21–end James 3
Thursday 21 July	G	Jeremiah 2.1–3, 7–8, 12–13 Psalm 36.5–10 Matthew 13.10–17	Psalm 37* 1 Samuel 17.1–30 Luke 23.56b—24.12	Psalms 39, **40** Ezekiel 34.1–16 James 4.1–12 *or:* 1st EP of Mary Magdalene: Psalm 139; Isaiah 25.1–9; 2 Corinthians 1.3–7
		Principal Service	**3rd Service**	**2nd Service**
Friday 22 July *Mary Magdalene*	W	Song of Solomon 3.1–4 Psalm 42.1–10 2 Corinthians 5.14–17 John 20.1–2, 11–18	MP Psalms 30, 32, 150 1 Samuel 16.14–end Luke 8.1–3	EP Psalm 63 Zephaniah 3.14–end Mark 15.40—16.7
		Holy Communion	**Morning Prayer**	**Evening Prayer**
Saturday 23 July *Bridget, abbess, 1373*	G	Jeremiah 7.1–11 Psalm 84.1–6	Psalms 41, **42**, 43 1 Samuel 17.55—18.16	Psalms 45, **46** Ezekiel 36.1–36

		1st Service	Holy Communion	2nd Service

Sunday 24 July — G
9th Sunday after Trinity
Proper 12

1st Service:
Psalm 95
Song of Solomon 2
or 1 Maccabees 2.[1–14] 15–22
1 Peter 4.7–14

Holy Communion:
Continuous:
Hosea 1.2–10
Psalm 85 [or 85.1–7]
Colossians 2.6–15 [16–19]
Luke 11.1–13

Related:
Genesis 18.20–32
Psalm 138
Colossians 2.6–15 [16–19]
Luke 11.1–13

2nd Service:
Psalm 88 [or **88**.1–10]
Genesis 42.1–25
1 Corinthians 10.1–24
HC Matthew 13.24–30 [31–43]
or: 1st EP of James the Apostle:
Psalm 144; Deuteronomy 30.11–end; Mark 5.21–end

Monday 25 July — R
James the Apostle

MP Psalms 7, 29, 117
2 Kings 1.9–15
Luke 9.46–56

Jeremiah 45.1–5 or Acts 11.27—12.2
Psalm 126
Acts 11.27—12.2 or 2 Corinthians 4.7–15
Matthew 20.20–28

EP Psalm 94
Jeremiah 26.1–15
Mark 1.14–20

Tuesday 26 July — Gw
Anne and Joachim, parents of the Blessed Virgin Mary
DEL week 17

Morning Prayer:
Psalms 48, 52
1 Samuel 20.1–17
Acts 1.15–end

Jeremiah 14.17–end
Psalm 79.8–end
Matthew 13.36–43
Lesser Festival eucharistic lectionary:
Zephaniah 3.14–18a; Psalm 127;
Romans 8.28–30; Matthew 13.16–17

Evening Prayer:
Psalm 50
Ezekiel 37.15–end
Mark 1.14–20

Wednesday 27 July — G
Brooke Foss Westcott, bishop, teacher of the faith, 1901

Psalm **119**.57–80
1 Samuel 20.18–end
Acts 2.1–21

Jeremiah 15.10, 16–end
Psalm 59.1–4, 18–end
Matthew 13.44–46

Psalms **59**, 60 (67)
Ezekiel 39.21–end
Mark 1.21–28

Thursday 28 July — G

Psalms 56, **57** (63*)
1 Samuel 21.1—22.5
Acts 2.22–36

Jeremiah 18.1–6
Psalm 146.1–5
Matthew 13.47–53

Psalms 61, **62**, 64
Ezekiel 43.1–12
Mark 1.29–end

Friday 29 July — Gw
Mary, Martha and Lazarus, companions of Our Lord

Psalms 51, 54
1 Samuel 22.6–end
Acts 2.37–end

Jeremiah 26.1–9
Psalm 69.4–10
Matthew 13.54–end
Lesser Festival eucharistic lectionary:
Isaiah 25.6–9; Psalm 49.5–10, 16;
Hebrews 2.10–15; John 12.1–8

Psalm 38
Ezekiel 44.4–16
Mark 2.1–12

Saturday 30 July — Gw
William Wilberforce, social reformer, Olaudah Equiano and Thomas Clarkson, anti-slavery campaigners, 1833, 1797 and 1846 (see p. 83)

Psalm 68
1 Samuel 23
Acts 3.1–10

Jeremiah 26.11–16, 24
Psalm 69.14–20
Matthew 14.1–12

Psalms 65, **66**
Ezekiel 47.1–12
Mark 2.13–22

Trinity 10

		Principal Service	3rd Service	2nd Service
Sunday	31 July **10th Sunday after Trinity** Proper 13	G	*Continuous:* Hosea 11.1–11 Psalm 107.1–9, 43 [or 107.1–9] *Related:* Ecclesiastes 1.2, 12–14; 2.18–23 Psalm 49.1–12 [or 49.1–9] Colossians 3.1–11 Luke 12.13–21	Psalm 106.1–10 Song of Solomon 5.2–end or 1 Maccabees 3.1–12 2 Peter 1.1–15	Psalm 107.1–32 [or 107.1–12] Genesis 50.4–end 1 Corinthians 14.1–19 HC Mark 6.45–52

			Holy Communion	Morning Prayer	Evening Prayer
Monday	1 August DEL week 18	G	Jeremiah 28 Psalm 119.89–96 Matthew 14.13–21 or 14.22–end	Psalm 71 1 Samuel 24 Acts 3.11–end	Psalms **72**, 75 Proverbs 1.1–19 Mark 2.23—3.6
Tuesday	2 August	G	Jeremiah 30.1–2, 12–15, 18–22 Psalm 102.16–21 Matthew 14.22–end or 15.1–2, 10–14	Psalm 73 1 Samuel 26 Acts 4.1–12	Psalm 74 Proverbs 1.20–end Mark 3.7–19a
Wednesday	3 August	G	Jeremiah 31.1–7 Psalm 121 Matthew 15.21–28	Psalm 77 1 Samuel 28.3–end Acts 4.13–31	Psalm **119.81–104** Proverbs 2 Mark 3.19b–end
Thursday	4 August *Jean-Baptiste Vianney, curé d'Ars, spiritual guide, 1859*	G	Jeremiah 31.31–34 Psalm 51.11–18 Matthew 16.13–23	Psalm **78.1–39*** 1 Samuel 31 Acts 4.32—5.11	Psalm **78.40–end*** Proverbs 3.1–26 Mark 4.1–20
Friday	5 August Oswald, king, martyr, 642 (see p. 79)	Gr	Nahum 2.1, 3, 3.1–3, 6–7 or Deuteronomy 32.35–36, 39, 41 Psalm 137.1–6 Matthew 16.24–28	Psalm 55 2 Samuel 1 Acts 5.12–26	Psalm 69 Proverbs 3.27—4.19 Mark 4.21–34 or: 1st EP of the Transfiguration of Our Lord Psalms 99, 110; Exodus 24.12–end; John 12.27–36a

			Principal Service	3rd Service	2nd Service
Saturday	6 August **Transfiguration of Our Lord**	*Gold or W*	Daniel 7.9–10, 13–14 Psalm 97 2 Peter 1.16–19 Luke 9.28–36	MP Psalms 27, 150 Ecclesiasticus 48.1–10 or 1 Kings 19.1–16 1 John 3.1–3	EP Psalm 72 Exodus 34.29–end 2 Corinthians 3

		Holy Communion		Morning Prayer	Evening Prayer
Sunday	**7 August** G **11th Sunday after Trinity** Proper 14	*Continuous:* Isaiah 1.1, 10–20 Psalm 50.1–8, 23–end [or 50.1–7] Hebrews 11.1–3, 8–16 Luke 12.32–40	*Related:* Genesis 15.1–6 Psalm 33.12–end [or 33.12–21] Hebrews 11.1–3, 8–16 Luke 12.32–40	Psalm 115 Song of Solomon 8.5–7 or 1 Maccabees 14.4–15 2 Peter 3.8–13	Psalms 108 [116] Isaiah 11.10—end of 12 2 Corinthians 1.1–22 HC Mark 7.24–30
Monday	**8 August** Gw Dominic, priest, founder of the Order of Preachers, 1221 (see p. 82) DEL week 19	Ezekiel 1.2–5, 24–end Psalm 148.1–4, 12–13 Matthew 17.22–end		Psalms 80, 82 2 Samuel 3.12–end Acts 6	Psalms 85, 86 Proverbs 8.1–21 Mark 5.1–20
Tuesday	**9 August** Gw Mary Sumner, founder of the Mothers' Union, 1921 (see p. 83)	Ezekiel 2.8—3.4 Psalm 119.65–72 Matthew 18.1–5, 10, 12–14		Psalms 87, **89.1–18** 2 Samuel 5.1–12 Acts 7.1–16	Psalm **89.19–end** Proverbs 8.22–end Mark 5.21–34
Wednesday	**10 August** Gr Laurence, deacon, martyr, 258	Ezekiel 9.1–7; 10.18–22 Psalm 113 Matthew 18.15–20		Psalm **119.105–128** 2 Samuel 6.1–19 Acts 7.17–43	Psalms 91, 93 Proverbs 9 Mark 5.35–end
Thursday	**11 August** Gw Clare of Assisi, founder of the Poor Clares, 1253 (see p. 82) *John Henry Newman, priest, 1890*	Ezekiel 12.1–12 Psalm 78.58–64 Matthew 18.21—19.1		Psalms 90, 92 2 Samuel 7.1–17 Acts 7.44–53	Psalm 94 Proverbs 10.1–12 Mark 6.1–13
Friday	**12 August** G	Ezekiel 16.1–15, 60–end Psalm 118.14–18 or *Canticle:* Song of Deliverance Matthew 19.3–12		Psalms 88 (95) 2 Samuel 7.18–end Acts 7.54—8.3	Psalm 102 Proverbs 11.1–12 Mark 6.14–29
Saturday	**13 August** Gw Jeremy Taylor, bishop, teacher of the faith, 1667 (see p. 80) *Florence Nightingale, nurse, social reformer, 1910* *Octavia Hill, social reformer, 1912*	Ezekiel 18.1–11a, 13b, 30, 32 Psalm 51.1–3, 15–17 Matthew 19.13–15		Psalms 96, **97**, 100 2 Samuel 9 Acts 8.4–25	Psalm 104 Proverbs 12.10–end Mark 6.30–44

53

Trinity 12

		Principal Service	3rd Service	2nd Service
Sunday 14 August 12th Sunday after Trinity Proper 15	G	*Continuous:* Isaiah 5.1–7; Psalm 80.1–2, 9–end [or 80.9–end] *Related:* Jeremiah 23.23–29; Psalm 82 Hebrews 11.29 —12.2 Luke 12.49–56	Psalm 119.33–48 Jonah 1 or Ecclesiasticus 3.1–15 2 Peter 3.14–end	Psalm 119.17–32 [or 119.17–24] Isaiah 28.9–22 2 Corinthians 8.1–9 HC Matthew 20.1–16 *or:* 1st EP of the Blessed Virgin Mary: Psalm 72; Proverbs 8.22–31; John 19.23–27
Monday 15 August The Blessed Virgin Mary	W	Isaiah 61.10–end or Revelation 11.19—12.6, 10 Psalm 45.10–end Galatians 4.4–7 Luke 1.46–55	MP Psalms 98, 138, 147.1–12 Isaiah 7.10–15 Luke 11.27–28	EP Psalm 132 Song of Solomon 2.1–7 Acts 1.6–14

		Holy Communion	Morning Prayer	Evening Prayer
Tuesday 16 August DEL week 20	G	Ezekiel 28.1–10 Psalm 107.1–3, 40, 43 Matthew 19.23–end	Psalm 106* (or 103) 2 Samuel 12.1–25 Acts 9.1–19a	Psalm 107* Proverbs 15.18–end Mark 7.1–13
Wednesday 17 August	G	Ezekiel 34.1–11 Psalm 23 Matthew 20.1–16	Psalms 110, 111, 112 2 Samuel 15.1–12 Acts 9.19b–31	Psalm 119.129–152 Proverbs 18.10–end Mark 7.14–23
Thursday 18 August	G	Ezekiel 36.23–28 Psalm 51.7–12 Matthew 22.1–14	Psalms 113, 115 2 Samuel 15.13–end Acts 9.32–end	Psalms 114, 116, 117 Proverbs 20.1–22 Mark 7.24–30
Friday 19 August	G	Ezekiel 37.1–14 Psalm 107.1–8 Matthew 22.34–40	Psalm 139 2 Samuel 16.1–14 Acts 10.1–16	Psalms 130, 131, 137 Proverbs 22.1–16 Mark 7.31–end
Saturday 20 August Bernard, abbot, teacher of the faith, 1153 (see p. 80) William and Catherine Booth, founders of the Salvation Army, 1912, 1890	Gw	Ezekiel 43.1–7 Psalm 85.7–end Matthew 23.1–12	Psalms 120, 121, 122 2 Samuel 17.1–23 Acts 10.17–33	Psalm 118 Proverbs 24.23–end Mark 8.1–10

		Principal Service		3rd Service	2nd Service
Sunday	**21 August** **13th Sunday after Trinity** Proper 16	G	*Continuous:* Jeremiah 1.4–10 Psalm 71.1–6	*Related:* Isaiah 58.9b–end Psalm 103.1–8 Hebrews 12.18–end Luke 13.10–17	Psalm 119.73–88 Jonah 2 or Ecclesiasticus 3.17–29 Revelation 1	Psalm 119.49–72 [or 119.49–56] Isaiah 30.8–21 2 Corinthians 9 *HC* Matthew 21.28–32
			Holy Communion		**Morning Prayer**	**Evening Prayer**
Monday	**22 August** DEL week 21	G	2 Thessalonians 1.1–5, 11–end Psalm 39.1–9 Matthew 23.13–22		Psalms 123, 124, 125, **126** 2 Samuel 18.1–18 Acts 10.34–end	Psalms **127**, 128, 129 Proverbs 25.1–14 Mark 8.11–21
Tuesday	**23 August**	G	2 Thessalonians 2.1–3a, 14–end Psalm 98 Matthew 23.23–26		Psalms **132**, 133 2 Samuel 18.19—19.8a Acts 11.1–18	Psalms (134,) **135** Proverbs 25.15–end Mark 8.22–26 *or:* 1st EP of Bartholomew the Apostle: Psalm 97; Isaiah 61.1–9; 2 Corinthians 6.1–10
			Principal Service		**3rd Service**	**2nd Service**
Wednesday	**24 August** Bartholomew the Apostle	R	Isaiah 43.8–13 or Acts 5.12–16 Psalm 145.1–7 Acts 5.12–16 or 1 Corinthians 4.9–15 Luke 22.24–30		*MP* Psalms 86, 117 Genesis 28.10–17 John 1.43–end	*EP* Psalms 91, 116 Ecclesiasticus 39.1–10 or: Deuteronomy 18.15–19 Matthew 10.1–22
			Holy Communion		**Morning Prayer**	**Evening Prayer**
Thursday	**25 August**	G	1 Corinthians 1.1–9 Psalm 145.1–7 Matthew 24.42–end		Psalms **143**, 146 2 Samuel 19.24–end Acts 12.1–17	Psalms **138**, 140, 141 Proverbs 27.1–22 Mark 9.2–13
Friday	**26 August**	G	1 Corinthians 1.17–25 Psalm 33.6–12 Matthew 25.1–13		Psalms 142, **144** 2 Samuel 23.1–7 Acts 12.18–end	Psalm **145** Proverbs 30.1–9, 24–31 Mark 9.14–29
Saturday	**27 August** Monica, mother of Augustine of Hippo, 387 (see p. 83)	Gw	1 Corinthians 1.26–end Psalm 33.12–15, 20–end Matthew 25.14–30		Psalm **147** 2 Samuel 24 Acts 13.1–12	Psalms **148**, 149, 150 Proverbs 31.10–end Mark 9.30–37

Trinity 14

		Principal Service	3rd Service	2nd Service
Sunday	**28 August** G **14th Sunday after Trinity** Proper 17	*Continuous:* Jeremiah 2.4–13 Psalm 81.1, 10–16 [or 81.1–11] *Related:* Ecclesiasticus 10.12–18 or Proverbs 25.6–7 Psalm 112 Hebrews 13.1–8, 15–16 Luke 14.1, 7–14	Psalm 119.161–end Jonah 3.1–9 or Ecclesiasticus 11.[7–17]18–28 Revelation 3.14–22	Psalm 119.81–96 [or 119.81–88] Isaiah 33.13–22 John 3.22–36
		Holy Communion	**Morning Prayer**	**Evening Prayer**
Monday	**29 August** Gr Beheading of John the Baptist DEL week 22	1 Corinthians 2.1–5 Psalm 33.12–21 Luke 4.16–30; *Lesser Festival eucharistic lectionary:* Jeremiah 1.4–10; Psalm 11; Hebrews 11.32—12.2; Matthew 14.1–12	Psalms 1, 2, 3 1 Kings 1.5–31 Acts 13.13–43	Psalms 4, 7 Wisdom 1 or 1 Chronicles 9.38–end Mark 9.38–end
Tuesday	**30 August** Gw John Bunyan, spiritual writer, 1688 (see p. 80)	1 Corinthians 2.10b–end Psalm 145.10–17 Luke 4.31–37	Psalms 5, 6 (8) 1 Kings 1.32—2.4; 2.10–12 Acts 13.44—14.7	Psalms 9, 10* Wisdom 2 or 1 Chronicles 13 Mark 10.1–16
Wednesday	**31 August** Gw Aidan, bishop, missionary, 651 (see p. 82)	1 Corinthians 3.1–9 Psalm 62 Luke 4.38–end	Psalm 119.1–32 1 Kings 3 Acts 14.8–end	Psalms 11, 12, 13 Wisdom 3.1–9 or 1 Chronicles 15.1—16.3 Mark 10.17–31
Thursday	**1 September** G *Giles, hermit, c.710*	1 Corinthians 3.18–end Psalm 24.1–6 Luke 5.1–11	Psalms 14, 15, 16 1 Kings 4.29—5.12 Acts 15.1–21	Psalm 18* Wisdom 4.7–end or 1 Chronicles 17 Mark 10.32–34
Friday	**2 September** G *Martyrs of Papua New Guinea, 1901, 1942*	1 Corinthians 4.1–5 Psalm 37.3–8 Luke 5.33–end	Psalms 17, 19 1 Kings 6.1, 11–28 Acts 15.22–35	Psalm 22 Wisdom 5.1–16 or 1 Chronicles 21.1—22.1 Mark 10.35–45
Saturday	**3 September** Gw Gregory the Great, bishop, teacher of the faith, 604 (see p. 80)	1 Corinthians 4.6–15 Psalm 145.18–end Luke 6.1–5	Psalms 20, 21, 23 1 Kings 8.1–30 Acts 15.36—16.5	Psalms 24, 25 Wisdom 5.17—6.11 or 1 Chronicles 22.2–end Mark 10.46–end

	Holy Communion	Morning Prayer	Evening Prayer
Sunday 4 September G **15th Sunday after Trinity** Proper 18	*Continuous:* Jeremiah 18.1–11 Psalm 139.1–5, 12–18 [or 139.1–7] Philemon 1–21 Luke 14.25–33 *Related:* Deuteronomy 30.15–end Psalm 1	Psalms 122, 123 Jonah 3.10—end of 4 or Ecclesiasticus 27.30 —28.9 Revelation 8.1–5	Psalms [120] 121 Isaiah 43.14—44.5 John 5.30–end
Monday 5 September G DEL week 23	1 Corinthians 5.1–8 Psalm 5.5–9a Luke 6.6–11	Psalms 27, **30** 1 Kings 8.31–62 Acts 16.6–24	Psalms 26, **28, 29** Wisdom 6.12–23 or 1 Chronicles 28.1–10 Mark 11.1–11
Tuesday 6 September G *Allen Gardiner, missionary, founder of the South American Mission Society, 1851*	1 Corinthians 6.1–11 Psalm 149.1–5 Luke 6.12–19	Psalms 32, **36** 1 Kings 8.63–9.9 Acts 16.25–end	Psalm **33** Wisdom 7.1–14 or 1 Chronicles 28.11–end Mark 11.12–26
Wednesday 7 September G	1 Corinthians 7.25–31 Psalm 45.11–end Luke 6.20–26	Psalm **34** 1 Kings 10.1–25 Acts 17.1–15	Psalm 1**19.33–56** Wisdom 7.15—8.4 or 1 Chronicles 29.1–9 Mark 11.27–end
Thursday 8 September Gw Birth of the Blessed Virgin Mary (see p. 79)	1 Corinthians 8.1–7, 11–end Psalm 139.1–9 Luke 6.27–38	Psalm **37*** 1 Kings 11.1–13 Acts 17.16–end	Psalms 39, **40** Wisdom 8.5–18 or 1 Chronicles 29.10–20 Mark 12.1–12
If the Festival of the Blessed Virgin Mary is transferred to 8 September, the provision (including 1st EP) for 15 August is used.			
Friday 9 September G *Charles Fuge Lowder, priest, 1880*	1 Corinthians 9.16–19, 22–end Psalm 84.1–6 Luke 6.39–42	Psalm **31** 1 Kings 11.26–end Acts 18.1–21	Psalm **35** Wisdom 8.21—end of 9 or 1 Chronicles 29.21–end Mark 12.13–17
Saturday 10 September G	1 Corinthians 10.14–22 Psalm 116.10–end Luke 6.43–end	Psalms 41, **42, 43** 1 Kings 12.1–24 Acts 18.22—19.7	Psalms 45, **46** Wisdom 10.15—11.10 or 2 Chronicles 1.1–13 Mark 12.18–27

		Principal Service		3rd Service	2nd Service
Sunday	**11 September** G 16th Sunday after Trinity Proper 19	*Continuous:* Jeremiah 4.11–12, 22–28 Psalm 14	*Related:* Exodus 32.7–14 Psalm 51.1–11 1 Timothy 1.12–17 Luke 15.1–10	Psalms 126, 127 Isaiah 44.24—45.8 Revelation 12.1–12	Psalms 124, 125 Isaiah 60 John 6.51–69
		Holy Communion		Morning Prayer	Evening Prayer
Monday	**12 September** G DEL week 24	1 Corinthians 11.17–26, 33 Psalm 40.7–11 Luke 7.1–10		Psalm **44** 1 Kings 12.25—13.10 Acts 19.8–20	Psalms **47**, 49 Wisdom 11.21—12.2 or 2 Chronicles 2.1–16 Mark 12.28–34
Tuesday	**13 September** Gw John Chrysostom, bishop, teacher of the faith, 407 (see p. 80)	1 Corinthians 12.12–14, 27–end Psalm 100 Luke 7.11–17		Psalms **48**, 52 1 Kings 13.11–end Acts 19.21–end	Psalm **50** Wisdom 12.12–21 or 2 Chronicles 3 Mark 12.35–end or: 1st EP of Holy Cross Day: Psalm 66; Isaiah 52.13—end of 53; Ephesians 2.11–end
		Principal Service		3rd Service	2nd Service
Wednesday	**14 September** R Holy Cross Day	Numbers 21.4–9 Psalm 22.23–28 Philippians 2.6–11 John 3.13–17		MP Psalms 2, 8, 146 Genesis 3.1–15 John 12.27–36a	EP Psalms 110, 150 Isaiah 63.1–16 1 Corinthians 1.18–25
		Holy Communion		Morning Prayer	Evening Prayer
Thursday	**15 September** Gr Cyprian, bishop, martyr, 258 (see p. 79)	1 Corinthians 15.1–11 Psalm 118; 1–2, 17–20 Luke 7.36–end		Psalms 56, **57** (63*) 1 Kings 18.1–20 Acts 20.17–end	Psalms 61, **62**, 64 Wisdom 16.15—17.1 or 2 Chronicles 6.1–21 Mark 13.14–23
Friday	**16 September** Gw Ninian, bishop, c.432 (see p. 82) *Edward Bouverie Pusey, priest, 1882*	1 Corinthians 15.12–20 Psalm 17.1–8 Luke 8.1–3		Psalms **51**, 54 1 Kings 18.21–end Acts 21.1–16	Psalm **38** Wisdom 18.6–19 or 2 Chronicles 6.22–end Mark 13.24–31
Saturday	**17 September** Gw Hildegard, abbess, visionary, 1179 (see p. 82)	1 Corinthians 15.35–37, 42–49 Psalm 30.1–5		Psalm **68** 1 Kings 19	Psalms 65, **66** Wisdom 19 or 2 Chronicles 7

Day		Holy Communion / Principal Service	Morning Prayer / 3rd Service	Evening Prayer / 2nd Service
Sunday	**18 September** **17th Sunday after Trinity** Proper 20	G	*Continuous:* Jeremiah 8.18—9.1 Psalm 79.1-9 *Related:* Amos 8.4-7 Psalm 113 1 Timothy 2.1-7 Luke 16.1-13	Psalms 130, 131 Isaiah 45.9-22 Revelation 14.1-5	Psalms [128] 129 Ezra 1 John 7.14-36
Monday	**19 September** *Theodore, archbishop, 690* DEL week 25	G	**Holy Communion** Proverbs 3.27-34 Psalm 15 Luke 8.16-18	**Morning Prayer** Psalm 71 1 Kings 21 Acts 21.37—22.21	**Evening Prayer** Psalms 72, 75 1 Maccabees 1.1-19 or 2 Chronicles 9.1-12 Mark 14.1-11
Tuesday	**20 September** John Coleridge Patteson, bishop, and companions, martyrs, 1871 (see p. 79)	Gr	Proverbs 21.1-6, 10-13 Psalm 119.1-8 Luke 8.19-21	Psalm 73 1 Kings 22.1-28 Acts 22.22—23.11	Psalm 74 1 Maccabees 1.20-40 or 2 Chronicles 10.1—11.4 Mark 14.12-25 *or:* 1st EP of Matthew, Apostle and Evangelist: Psalm 34; Isaiah 33.13-17; Matthew 6.19-end
Wednesday	**21 September** Matthew, Apostle and Evangelist	R	**Principal Service** Proverbs 3.13-18 Psalm 119.65-72 2 Corinthians 4.1-6 Matthew 9.9-13	**3rd Service** MP Psalms 49, 117 1 Kings 19.15-end 2 Timothy 3.14-end	**2nd Service** EP Psalm 119.33-40, 89-96 Ecclesiastes 5.4-12 Matthew 19.16-end
Thursday	**22 September**	G	**Holy Communion** Ecclesiastes 1.2-11 Psalm 90.1-6 Luke 9.7-9	**Morning Prayer** Psalm 78.1-39* 2 Kings 1.2-17 Acts 24.1-23	**Evening Prayer** Psalm **78.40-end*** 1 Maccabees 2.1-28 or 2 Chronicles 13.1—14.1 Mark 14.43-52
Friday	**23 September**	G	Ecclesiastes 3.1-11 Psalm 144.1-4 Luke 9.18-22	Psalm 55 2 Kings 2.1-18 Acts 24.24—25.12	Psalm 69 1 Maccabees 2.29-48 or 2 Chronicles 14.2-end Mark 14.53-65
Saturday	**24 September**	G	Ecclesiastes 11.9—12.8 Psalm 90.1-2, 12-end Luke 9.43b-45	Psalms 76, 79 2 Kings 4.1-37 Acts 25.13-end	Psalms 81, **84** 1 Maccabees 2.49-end or 2 Chronicles 15.1-15 Mark 14.66-end

Trinity 18

	Principal Service	3rd Service	2nd Service
Sunday **25 September** G 18th Sunday after Trinity Proper 21	Continuous: Jeremiah 32.1–3a, 6–15; Psalm 91.1–6, 14–end [or 91.11–end]; Related: Amos 6.1a, 4–7; Psalm 146; 1 Timothy 6.6–19; Luke 16.19–end	Psalm 132; Isaiah 48.12–end; Luke 11.37–end	Psalms 134, 135 [or 135.1–14]; Nehemiah 2; John 8.31–38, 48–end

	Holy Communion	Morning Prayer	Evening Prayer
Monday **26 September** G Wilson Carlile, founder of the Church Army, 1942; DEL week 26	Job 1.6–end; Psalm 17.1–11; Luke 9.46–50	Psalms 80, 82; 2 Kings 5; Acts 26.1–23	Psalms 85, 86; 1 Maccabees 3.1–26 or 2 Chronicles 17.1–12; Mark 15.1–15
Tuesday **27 September** Gw Vincent de Paul, founder of the Lazarists, 1660 (see p. 82)	Job 3.1–3, 11–17, 20–23; Psalm 88.1–19; Luke 9.51–56	Psalms 87, 89.1–18; 2 Kings 6.1–23; Acts 26.24–end	Psalm 89.19–end; 1 Maccabees 3.27–41 or 2 Chronicles 18.1–27; Mark 15.16–32
Wednesday **28 September** G Ember Day	Job 9.1–12, 14–16; Psalm 88.1–6, 11; Luke 9.57–end	Psalm 119.105–128; 2 Kings 9.1–16; Acts 27.1–26	Psalms 91, 93; 1 Maccabees 3.42–end or 2 Chronicles 18.28—end of 19; Mark 15.33–41 or: 1st EP of Michael and All Angels: Psalm 91; 2 Kings 6.8–17; Matthew 18.1–6,10

	Principal Service	3rd Service	2nd Service
Thursday **29 September** W Michael and All Angels	Genesis 28.10–17 or Revelation 12.7–12; Psalm 103.19–end; Revelation 12.7–12 or Hebrews 1.5–end; John 1.47–end	MP Psalms 34, 150; Tobit 12.6–end or Daniel 12.1–4; Acts 12.1–11	EP Psalms 138, 148; Daniel 10.4–end; Revelation 5

	Holy Communion	Morning Prayer	Evening Prayer
Friday **30 September** G Jerome, translator, teacher of the faith, 420; Ember Day	Job 38.1, 12–21, 40.3–5; Psalm 139.6–11; Luke 10.13–16	Psalm 88 (95); 2 Kings 12.1–19; Acts 28.1–16	Psalm 102; 1 Maccabees 4.26–35 or 2 Chronicles 22.10—end of 23; Mark 16.1–8
Saturday **1 October** G Remigius, bishop, 533; Anthony Ashley Cooper (Earl of Shaftesbury),	Job 42.1–3, 6, 12–end; Psalm 119.169–end; Luke 10.17–24	Psalms 96, 97, 100; 2 Kings 17.1–23; Acts 28.17–end	Psalm 104; 1 Maccabees 4.36–end or 2 Chronicles 24.1–22

			Third Service	Second Service / Holy Communion		
Sunday	2 October 19th Sunday after Trinity Proper 22	G	Psalm 141 Isaiah 49.13–23 Luke 12.1–12	*Continuous:* Lamentations 1.1–6 *Canticle:* Lamentations 3.19–26 or Psalm 137 [or 137.1–6] 2 Timothy 1.1–14 Luke 17.5–10	*Related:* Habakkuk 1.1–4; 2.1–4 Psalm 37.1–9	

			Holy Communion	Morning Prayer	Evening Prayer
Monday	3 October *George Bell, bishop, ecumenist, peacemaker,* *1958* DEL week 27	G	Galatians 1.6–12 Psalm 111.1–6 Luke 10.25–37	Psalms 98, 99, 101 2 Kings 17.24–end Philippians 1.1–11	Psalm 105* (or 103) 1 Maccabees 6.1–17 or 2 Chronicles 26.1–21 John 13.1–11
Tuesday	4 October *Francis of Assisi, friar, deacon, 1226* (see p. 82)	Gw	Galatians 1.13–end Psalm 139.1–9 Luke 10.38–end	Psalm 106* (or 103) 2 Kings 18.1–12 Philippians 1.12–end	Psalm 107* 1 Maccabees 6.18–47 or 2 Chronicles 28 John 13.12–20
Wednesday	5 October	G	Galatians 2.1–2, 7–14 Psalm 117 Luke 11.1–4	Psalms 110, 111, 112 2 Kings 18.13–end Philippians 2.1–13	Psalm **119.129–152** 1 Maccabees 7.1–20 or 2 Chronicles 29.1–19 John 13.21–30
Thursday	6 October *William Tyndale, translator, martyr, 1536* (see p. 79)	Gr	Galatians 3.1–5 *Canticle:* Benedictus Luke 11.5–13	Psalms 113, **115** 2 Kings 19.1–19 Philippians 2.14–end	Psalms 114, **116**, 117 1 Maccabees 7.21–end or 2 Chronicles 29.20–end John 13.31–end
Friday	7 October	G	Galatians 3.7–14 Psalm 111.4–end Luke 11.15–26	Psalm **139** 2 Kings 19.20–36 Philippians 3.1—4.1	Psalms **130**, **131**, 137 1 Maccabees 9.1–22 or 2 Chronicles 30 John 14.1–14
Saturday	8 October	G	Galatians 3.22–end Psalm 105.1–7 Luke 11.27–28	Psalms 120, **121**, 122 2 Kings 20 Philippians 4.2–end	Psalm **118** 1 Maccabees 13.41–end, 14.4–15 or 2 Chronicles 32.1–22 John 14.15–end

		Principal Service		3rd Service	2nd Service
Sunday	**9 October** G **20th Sunday after Trinity** Proper 23	*Continuous:* Jeremiah 29.1, 4–7 Psalm 66.1–11	*Related:* 2 Kings 5.1–3, 7–15c Psalm 111	Psalm 143 Isaiah 50.4–10 Luke 13.22–30	Psalm 144 Nehemiah 6.1–16 John 15.12–end
		2 Timothy 2.8–15 Luke 17.11–19			
		Holy Communion		**Morning Prayer**	**Evening Prayer**
Monday	**10 October** Gw Paulinus, bishop, missionary, 644 (see p. 82) *Thomas Traherne, poet, spiritual writer, 1674* DEL week 28	Galatians 4.21–24, 26–27, 31; 5.1 Psalm 113 Luke 11.29–32		Psalms 123, 124, 125, **126** 2 Kings 21.1–18 1 Timothy 1.1–17	Psalms 127, 128, 129 2 Maccabees 4.7–17 or 2 Chronicles 33.1–13 John 15.1–11
Tuesday	**11 October** G *Ethelburga, abbess, 675* *James the Deacon, companion of Paulinus,* *7th cent.*	Galatians 5.1–6 Psalm 119.41–48 Luke 11.37–41		Psalms **132**, 133 2 Kings 22.1—23.3 1 Timothy 1.18–end of 2	Psalms (134), **135** 2 Maccabees 6.12–end or 2 Chronicles 34.1–18 John 15.12–17
Wednesday	**12 October** Gw Wilfrid, bishop, missionary, 709 (see p. 82) *Elizabeth Fry, prison reformer, 1845* *Edith Cavell, nurse, 1915*	Galatians 5.18–end Psalm 1 Luke 11.42–46		Psalm **119.153–end** 2 Kings 23.4–25 1 Timothy 3	Psalm **136** 2 Maccabees 7.1–19 or 2 Chronicles 34.19–end John 15.18–end
Thursday	**13 October** Gw Edward the Confessor, king, 1066 (see p. 83)	Ephesians 1.1–10 Psalm 98.1–4 Luke 11.47–end		Psalms 143, 146 2 Kings 23.36—24.17 1 Timothy 4	Psalms **138**, 140, 141 2 Maccabees 7.20–41 or 2 Chronicles 35.1–19 John 16.1–15
Friday	**14 October** G	Ephesians 1.11–14 Psalm 33.1–6, 12 Luke 12.1–7		Psalms 142, **144** 2 Kings 24.18—25.12 1 Timothy 5.1–16	Psalm **145** Tobit 1 or 2 Chronicles 35.20—36.10 John 16.16–22
Saturday	**15 October** Gw Teresa of Avila, teacher of the faith, 1582 (see p. 80)	Ephesians 1.15–end Psalm 8 Luke 12.8–12		Psalm **147** 2 Kings 25.22–end 1 Timothy 5.17–end	Psalms **148**, 149, 150 Tobit 2 or 2 Chronicles 36.11–end John 16.23–end

Day		Colour	Principal Service / Holy Communion	3rd Service / Morning Prayer	2nd Service / Evening Prayer
Sunday	**16 October** **21st Sunday after Trinity** Proper 24	G	Continuous: Jeremiah 31.27–34 Psalm 119.97–104 *Related:* Genesis 32.22–31 Psalm 121 2 Timothy 3.14—4.5 Luke 18.1–8	Psalm 147 Isaiah 54.1–14 Luke 13.31–end	Psalms [146] 149 Nehemiah 8.9–end John 16.1–11
			Holy Communion	**Morning Prayer**	**Evening Prayer**
Monday	**17 October** Ignatius, bishop, martyr, c.107 (see p. 79) DEL week 29	Gr	Ephesians 2.1–10 Psalm 100 Luke 12.13–21	Psalms 1, 2, 3 Judith 4 or Exodus 22.21–27, 23.1–17 1 Timothy 6.1–10	Psalms **4**, 7 Tobit 3 or Micah 1.1–9 John 17.1–5 or: 1st EP of Luke the Evangelist: Psalm 33; Hosea 6.1–3; 2; Timothy 3.10–end
			Principal Service	**3rd Service**	**2nd Service**
Tuesday	**18 October** *Luke the Evangelist*	R	Isaiah 35.3–6 or Acts 16.6–12*a* Psalm 147.1–7 2 Timothy 4.5–17 Luke 10.1–9	MP Psalms 145, 146 Isaiah 55 Luke 1.1–4	EP Psalm 103 Ecclesiasticus 38.1–14 or Isaiah 61.1–6 Colossians 4.7–end
			Holy Communion	**Morning Prayer**	**Evening Prayer**
Wednesday	**19 October** Henry Martyn, translator, missionary, 1812 (see p. 82)	Gw	Ephesians 3.2–12 Psalm 98 Luke 12.39–48	Psalms **119**.1–32 Judith 6.10—7.7 or Leviticus 8 2 Timothy 1.1–14	Psalms **11**, 12, 13 Tobit 5.1—6.1*a* or Micah 3 John 17.20–end
Thursday	**20 October**	G	Ephesians 3.14–end Psalm 33.1–6 Luke 12.49–53	Psalms 14, **15**, 16 Judith 7.19–end or Leviticus 9 2 Timothy 1.15—2.13	Psalm 18* Tobit 6.1*b*–end or Micah 4.1—5.1 John 18.1–11
Friday	**21 October**	G	Ephesians 4.1–6 Psalm 24.1–6 Luke 12.54–end	Psalms 17, **19** Judith 8.9–end or Leviticus 16.2–24 2 Timothy 2.14–end	Psalm **22** Tobit 7 or Micah 5.2–end John 18.12–27
Saturday	**22 October**	G	Ephesians 4.7–16 Psalm 122 Luke 13.1–9	Psalms 20, 21, **23** Judith 9 or Leviticus 17 2 Timothy 3	Psalms **24**, 25 Tobit 8 or Micah 6 John 18.28–end

63

Last after Trinity

64

		Principal Service	3rd Service	2nd Service
Sunday	**23 October** **Last Sunday after Trinity** Proper 25	G *Continuous:* Joel 2.23–end Psalm 65 [or 65.1–7] *Related:* Ecclesiasticus 35.12–end or Jeremiah 14.7–10, 19–end Psalm 84.1–7 2 Timothy 4.6–8, 16–18 Luke 18.9–14	Psalm 119.105–128 Isaiah 59.9–20 Luke 14.1–14	Psalm 119.1–16 Ecclesiastes 11, 12 2 Timothy 2.1–7 HC Matthew 22.34–end

or, if the date of dedication of a church is not known, the Dedication Festival *(Gold or W) may be celebrated today or on 4 October, or on a suitable date chosen locally (see p. 78)*

		Principal Service	3rd Service	2nd Service
or Sunday	**23 October** **Bible Sunday**	G Isaiah 45.22–end Psalm 119.129–136 Romans 15.1–6 Luke 4.16–24	Psalm 119.105–128 1 Kings 22.1–17 Romans 15.4–13 or Luke 14.1–14	Psalm 119.1–16 Jeremiah 36.9–end Romans 10.5–17 HC Matthew 22.34–end

		Holy Communion	Morning Prayer	Evening Prayer
Monday	**24 October** DEL week 30	G Ephesians 4.32—5.8 Psalm 1 Luke 13.10–17	Psalms 27, **30** Judith 10 or Leviticus 19.1–18, 30–end 2 Timothy 4.1–8	Psalms 26, **28**, 29 Tobit 9 or Micah 7.1–7 John 19.1–16
Tuesday	**25 October** *Crispin and Crispinian, martyrs, c.287*	G Ephesians 5.21–end Psalm 128 Luke 13.18–21	Psalms 32, **36** Judith 11 or Leviticus 23.1–22 2 Timothy 4.9–end	Psalm **33** Tobit 10 or Micah 7.8–end John 19.17–30
Wednesday	**26 October** Alfred, king, scholar, 899 (see p. 83) *Cedd, abbot, bishop, 664*	Gw Ephesians 6.1–9 Psalm 145.10–20 Luke 13.22–30	Psalm **34** Judith 12 or Leviticus 23.23–end Titus 1	Psalm **119.33–56** Tobit 11 or Habakkuk 1.1–11 John 19.31–end
Thursday	**27 October**	G Ephesians 6.10–20 Psalm 144.1–2, 9–11 Luke 13.31–end	Psalm **37*** Judith 13 or Leviticus 24.1–9 Titus 2	Psalms 39, **40** Tobit 12 or Habakkuk 1.12—2.5 John 20.1–10 or: 1st EP of Simon and Jude, Apostles: Psalms 124, 125, 126; Deuteronomy 32.1–4; John 14.15–26

		Principal Service	3rd Service	2nd Service
Friday	**28 October** Simon and Jude, Apostles	R Isaiah 28.14–16 Psalm 119.89–96 Ephesians 2.19–end John 15.17–end	*MP* Psalms 116, 117 Wisdom 5.1–16 or Isaiah 45.18–end Luke 6.12–16	*EP* Psalm 119.1–16 1 Maccabees 2.42–66 or Jeremiah 3.11–18 Jude 1–4, 17–end

All Saints' Day is celebrated either on Tuesday 1 November or Sunday 30 October; if the latter there may be a supplementary celebration on 1 November.

		Holy Communion	Morning Prayer	Evening Prayer
Saturday	**29 October** *James Hannington, bishop, martyr, 1885* (see p. 79)	Gr	Psalms 41, **42**, 43 Judith 15.14—end of 16 *or* Numbers 6.1–5, 21—end Philemon	Psalms 45, **46** Tobit 14.2—end *or* Habakkuk 3.2—19a John 20.19—end
		Philippians 1.18–26 Psalm 42.1–7 Luke 14.1, 7–11		*or, if All Saints' Day is celebrated on Sunday 30 October only:* **1st EP of All Saints' Day:** Psalms 1, 5; Ecclesiasticus 44.1–15 *or* Isaiah 40.27—end; Revelation 19.6–10

		Principal Service	3rd Service	2nd Service
Sunday	*If All Saints' Day is celebrated on Tuesday 1 November:*			
	30 October R/G **4th Sunday before Advent**	Isaiah 1.10–18 Psalm 32.1–8 2 Thessalonians 1 Luke 19.1–10	Psalm 87 Job 26 Colossians 1.9–14	Psalm 145 [or 145.1–9] Lamentations 3.22–33 John 11.[1–31] 32–44
	If All Saints' Day is celebrated on Sunday 30 October:			
or Sunday	**30 October** Gold or W **All Saints' Day**	Daniel 7.1–3,15–18 Psalm 149 Ephesians 1.11—end Luke 6.20–31	MP Psalms 15, 84, 149 Isaiah 35.1–9 Luke 9.18–27	EP Psalms 148, 150 Isaiah 65.17—end Hebrews 11.32—12.2

		Holy Communion	Morning Prayer	Evening Prayer
Monday	**31 October** R/G *Martin Luther, reformer, 1546* DEL week 31	Philippians 2.1–4 Psalm 131 Luke 14.12–14	Psalms **2**, 146 *or* **44** Daniel 1 Revelation 1	Psalms 92, 96, 97 *or* **47**, 49 Isaiah 1.1–20 Matthew 1.18—end
				or, if All Saints' Day is celebrated on Tuesday 1 November only: **1st EP of All Saints' Day:** Psalms 1, 5; Ecclesiasticus 44.1–15 *or* Isaiah 40.27—end; Revelation 19.6–10

All Saints' Day

		Principal Service	3rd Service	2nd Service
			Morning Prayer	Evening Prayer
Tuesday 1 November All Saints' Day	Gold or W	Daniel 7.1–3,15–18 Psalm 149 Ephesians 1.11–end Luke 6.20–31	MP Psalms 15, 84, 149 Isaiah 35.1–9 Luke 9.18–27	EP Psalms 148, 150 Isaiah 65.17–end Hebrews 11.32—12.2

If All Saints' Day is celebrated on Sunday 30 October only:

			Holy Communion	
or **Tuesday 1 November**	R/G		Psalms 5, 147.1–12 or **48**, 52 Daniel 2.1–24 Revelation 2.1–11	Psalms 98, 99, **100** or **50** Isaiah 1.21–end Matthew 2.1–15

If All Saints' Day is celebrated on Tuesday 1 November in addition to Sunday 30 October:

		Principal Service	3rd Service	2nd Service
or **Tuesday 1 November** All Saints' Day	Gold or W	Isaiah 56.3–8 or 2 Esdras 2.42–end Psalm 33.1–5 Hebrews 12.18–24 Matthew 5.1–12	MP Psalms 111, 112, 117 Wisdom 5.1–16 or Jeremiah 31.31–34 2 Corinthians 4.5–12	EP Psalm 145 Isaiah 66.20–23 Colossians 1.9–14
Wednesday 2 November Commemoration of the Faithful Departed (All Souls' Day)	Rp/Gp	Philippians 2.12–18 Psalm 27.1–5 Luke 14.25–33 *Lesser Festival eucharistic lectionary:* Lamentations 3.17–26, 31–33 or Wisdom 3.1–9; Psalm 23 or 27.1–6,16–end; Romans 5.5–11 or 1 Peter 1.3–9; John 5.19–25 or John 6.37–40	Psalms 9, 147.13–end or **119.57–80** Daniel 2.25–end Revelation 2.12–end	Psalms 111, **112**, 116 or **59**, 60, (67) Isaiah 2.1–11 Matthew 2.16–end
Thursday 3 November Richard Hooker, priest, teacher of the faith, 1600 (p. 80); *Martin of Porres, friar, 1639*	Rw/Gw	Philippians 3.3–8a Psalm 105.1–7 Luke 15.1–10	Psalms 11, **15**, 148 or 56, **57** (63) Daniel 3.1–18 Revelation 3.1–13	Psalm **118** or 61, **62**, 64 Isaiah 2.12–end Matthew 3
Friday 4 November	R/G	Philippians 3.17—4.1 Psalm 122 Luke 16.1–8	Psalms 16, 149 or **51**, 54 Daniel 3.19–end Revelation 3.14–end	Psalms 137, 138, **143** or 38 Isaiah 3.1–15 Matthew 4.1–11
Saturday 5 November	R/G	Philippians 4.10–19 Psalm 112 Luke 16.9–15	Psalms **18.31–end**, 150 or **68** Daniel 4.1–18 Revelation 4	Psalm **145** or 65, **66** Isaiah 4.2–5.7 Matthew 4.12–22

		Principal Service	3rd Service	2nd Service
Sunday	**6 November** R/G **3rd Sunday before Advent**	Job 19.23–27a Psalm 17.1–9 [or 17.1–8] 2 Thessalonians 2.1–5, 13–17 Luke 20.27–38	Psalms 20, 90 Isaiah 2.1–5 James 3.13–end	Psalm 40 1 Kings 3.1–15 Romans 8.31–end HC Matthew 22.15–22
		Holy Communion	**Morning Prayer**	**Evening Prayer**
Monday	**7 November** Rw/Gw Willibrord, bishop, 739 (see p. 82) DEL week 32	Titus 1.1–9 Psalm 24.1–6 Luke 17.1–6	Psalms 19, **20**, or **71** Daniel 4.19–end Revelation 5	Psalm **34** or **72**, 75 Isaiah 5.8–24 Matthew 4.23—5.12
Tuesday	**8 November** Rw/Gw Saints and Martyrs of England	Titus 2.1–8, 11–14 Psalm 37.3–5, 30–32 Luke 17.7–10 Lesser Festival eucharistic lectionary: Isaiah 61.4–9 or Ecclesiasticus 44.1–15; Psalm 15; Revelation 19.5–10; John 17.18–23	Psalms **21**, 24 or **73** Daniel 5.1–12 Revelation 6	Psalms 36, **40** or **74** Isaiah 5.25–end Matthew 5.13–20
Wednesday	**9 November** R/G Margery Kempe, mystic, c.1440	Titus 3.1–7 Psalm 23 Luke 17.11–19	Psalms **23**, 25 or **77** Daniel 5.13–end Revelation 7.1–4, 9–end	Psalm **37** or 119.**81**–104 Isaiah 6 Matthew 5.21–37
Thursday	**10 November** Rw/Gw Leo the Great, bishop, teacher of the faith, 461 (see p. 81)	Philemon 7–20 Psalm 146.4–end Luke 17.20–25	Psalms **26**, 27 or **78.1–39*** Daniel 6 Revelation 8	Psalms 42, **43** or **78.40–end*** Isaiah 7.1–17 Matthew 5.38–end
Friday	**11 November** Rw/Gw Martin, bishop, c.397 (see p. 81)	2 John 4–9 Psalm 119.1–8 Luke 17.26–end	Psalms 28, **32** or **55** Daniel 7.1–14 Revelation 9.1–12	Psalm **31** or **69** Isaiah 8.1–15 Matthew 6.1–18
Saturday	**12 November** R/G	3 John 5–8 Psalm 112 Luke 18.1–8	Psalm **33** or 76, **79** Daniel 7.15–end Revelation 9.13–end	Psalms 84, **86** or 81, **84** Isaiah 8.1–15 Matthew 6.19–end

		Principal Service	3rd Service	2nd Service
Sunday	**13 November** *R/G* **2nd Sunday before Advent** *Remembrance Sunday*	Malachi 4.1–2a Psalm 98 2 Thessalonians 3.6–13 Luke 21.5–19	Psalm 132 1 Samuel 16.1–13 Matthew 13.44–52	Psalm [93] 97 Daniel 6 Matthew 13.1–9, 18–23
		Holy Communion	*Morning Prayer*	*Evening Prayer*
Monday	**14 November** *R/G* *Samuel Seabury, bishop, 1796* DEL week 33	Revelation 1.1–4, 2.1–5 Psalm 1 Luke 18.35–end	Psalms 46, **47** or **80**, 82 Daniel 8.1–14 Revelation 10	Psalms 70, **71** or **85**, 86 Isaiah 9.8—10.4 Matthew 7.1–12
Tuesday	**15 November** *R/G*	Revelation 3.1–6, 14–end Psalm 15 Luke 19.1–10	Psalms 48, **52** or 87, **89.1–18** Daniel 8.15–end Revelation 11.1–14	Psalms **67**, 72 or **89.19—end** Isaiah 10.5–19 Matthew 7.13–end
Wednesday	**16 November** *Rw/Gw* Margaret, queen, philanthropist, 1093 (see p. 83) *Edmund Rich, archbishop, 1240*	Revelation 4 Psalm 150 Luke 19.11–28	Psalms **56**, 57 or **119.105–128** Daniel 9.1–19 Revelation 11.15–end	Psalm 73 or **91**, 93 Isaiah 10.20–32 Matthew 8.1–13
Thursday	**17 November** *Rw/Gw* Hugh, bishop, 1200 (see p. 81)	Revelation 5.1–10 Psalm 149.1–5 Luke 19.41–44	Psalms 61, **62** or 90, **92** Daniel 9.20–end Revelation 12	Psalms 74, **76** or **94** Isaiah 10.33—11.9 Matthew 8.14–22
Friday	**18 November** *Rw/Gw* Elizabeth, princess, philanthropist, 1231 (see p. 83)	Revelation 10.8–end Psalm 119.65–72 Luke 19.45–end	Psalms **63**, 65 or 88, (95) Daniel 10.1—11.1 Revelation 13.1–10	Psalm 77 or **102** Isaiah 11.10—end of 12 Matthew 8.23–end
Saturday	**19 November** *Rw/Gw* Hilda, abbess, 680 (see p. 82) *Mechtild, béguine, mystic, 1280*	Revelation 11.4–12 Psalm 144.1–9 Luke 20.27–40	Psalm **78.**1–39 or 96, **97**, 100 Daniel 12 Revelation 13.11–end	Psalm 78.40–**end** or **104** Isaiah 13.1–13 Matthew 9.1–17 *or:* 1st EP of Christ the King: Psalms 99, 100; Isaiah 10.33—11.9; 1 Timothy 6.11–16

Day	Date / Commemoration		Morning Prayer	Holy Communion	Evening Prayer
Sunday	**20 November** Christ the King *Sunday next before Advent*	R/W	*MP* Psalms 29, 110 Zechariah 6.9-end Revelation 11.15-18	Jeremiah 23.1-6 Psalm 46 Colossians 1.11-20 Luke 23.33-43	*EP* Psalm 72 [or 72.1-7] 1 Samuel 8.4-20 John 18.33-37
			Morning Prayer	Holy Communion	Evening Prayer
Monday	**21 November** DEL week 34	R/G	Psalms 92, **96** or **98**, 99, 101 Isaiah 40.1-11 Revelation 14.1-13	Revelation 14.1-5 Psalm 24.1-6 Luke 21.1-4	Psalms 80, 81 or **105*** (or 103) Isaiah 14.3-20 Matthew 9.18-34
Tuesday	**22 November** *Cecilia, martyr, c.230*	R/G	Psalms **97**, 98, 100 or **106*** (or 103) Isaiah 40.12-26 Revelation 14.14—end of 15	Revelation 14.14-19 Psalm 96 Luke 21.5-11	Psalms 99, **101** or **107*** Isaiah 17 Matthew 9.35—10.15
Wednesday	**23 November** *Clement, bishop, martyr, c.100 (see p. 79)*	R/Gr	Psalms 110, 111, **112** or 110, **111**, 112 Isaiah 40.27—41.7 Revelation 16.1-11	Revelation 15.1-4 Psalm 98 Luke 21.12-19	Psalms 121, **122**, 123, 124 or 119.**129-152** Isaiah 19 Matthew 10.16-33
Thursday	**24 November**	R/G	Psalms **125**, 126, 127, 128 or 113, **115** Isaiah 41.8-20 Revelation 16.12-end	Revelation 18.1-2, 21-23; 19.1-3, 9 Psalm 100 Luke 21.20-28	Psalms 131, 132, **133** or 114, **116**, 117 Isaiah 21.1-12 Matthew 10.34—11.1
Friday	**25 November** *Catherine, martyr, 4th cent.* *Isaac Watts, hymn writer, 1748*	R/G	Psalm **139** or **139**† Isaiah 41.21—42.9 Revelation 17 † *The two Psalm cycles coincide at this point*	Revelation 20.1-4, 11—21.2 Psalm 84.1-6 Luke 21.29-33	Psalms 146, 147 or **130**, **131**, 137 Isaiah 22.1-14 Matthew 11.2-19
Saturday	**26 November**	R/G	Psalm **145** or 120, **121**, 122 Isaiah 42.10-17 Revelation 18	Revelation 22.1-7 Psalm 95.1-7 Luke 21.34-36	Psalms 148, 149, **150** or **118** Isaiah 24 Matthew 11.20-end

¶ Additional Weekday Lectionary

This Additional Weekday Lectionary provides two readings for each day of the year, except for Sundays, Principal Feasts and other Principal Holy Days, Holy Week and Festivals (for which the readings provided in the main body of this lectionary are used). The readings for 'first evensongs' in the main body of the lectionary are used on the eves of Principal Feasts and may be used on the eves of Festivals. This lectionary is intended particularly for use in those places of worship that attract occasional rather than daily worshippers, and can be used either at Morning or Evening Prayer. Psalmody is not provided and should be taken from the daily provision earlier in this volume.

		29 November – Advent 1	
Monday	**30 November**	Andrew the Apostle – see p. 10	
Tuesday	**1 December**	Zephaniah 3.14–end	1 Thessalonians 4.13–end
Wednesday	**2 December**	Isaiah 65.17—66.2	Matthew 24.1–14
Thursday	**3 December**	Micah 5.2–5a	John 3.16–21
Friday	**4 December**	Isaiah 66.18–end	Luke 13.22–30
Saturday	**5 December**	Micah 7.8–15	Romans 15.30—16.7, 25–
		6 December – Advent 2	
Monday	**7 December**	Jeremiah 7.1–11	Philippians 4.4–9
Tuesday	**8 December**	Daniel 7.9–14	Matthew 24.15–28
Wednesday	**9 December**	Amos 9.11–end	Romans 13.8–end
Thursday	**10 December**	Jeremiah 23.5–8	Mark 11.1–11
Friday	**11 December**	Jeremiah 33.14–22	Luke 21.25–36
Saturday	**12 December**	Zechariah 14.4–11	Revelation 22.1–7
		13 December – Advent 3	
Monday	**14 December**	Isaiah 40.1–11	Matthew 3.1–12
Tuesday	**15 December**	Lamentations 3.22–33	1 Corinthians 1.1–9
Wednesday	**16 December**	Joel 3.9–16	Matthew 24.29–35
Thursday	**17 December**	Ecclesiasticus 24.1–9 or Proverbs 8.22–31	1 Corinthians 2.1–13
Friday	**18 December**	Exodus 3.1–6	Acts 7.20–36
Saturday	**19 December**	Isaiah 11.1–9	Romans 15.7–13
		20 December – Advent 4	
Monday	**21 December**	Numbers 24.15b–19	Revelation 22.10–21
Tuesday	**22 December**	Jeremiah 30.7–11a	Acts 4.1–12
Wednesday	**23 December**	Isaiah 7.10–15	Matthew 1.18–23
Thursday	**24 December**	*At Evening Prayer the readings for* **Christmas Eve** *are used. At other services, the following readings are used* Isaiah 29.13–18	1 John 4.7–16
Friday	**25 December**	**Christmas Day** – see p. 13	
Saturday	**26 December**	Stephen, deacon, martyr – see p. 13	
		27 December – John, Apostle and Evangelist / Christmas 1	
Monday	**28 December**	The Holy Innocents – see p. 14	
Tuesday	**29 December**	Micah 1.1–4; 2.12–13 or John, Apostle and Evangelist – see p. 14	Luke 2.1–7
Wednesday	**30 December**	Isaiah 9.2–7	John 8.12–20
Thursday	**31 December**	Ecclesiastes 3.1–13 or 1st EP of Naming and Circumcision of Jesus	Revelation 21.1–8
Friday	**1 January**	Naming and Circumcision of Jesus – see p. 15	
Saturday	**2 January**	Isaiah 66.6–14	Matthew 12.46–50
		If, for pastoral reasons, **The Epiphany** *is celebrated on Sunday 3 January the readings for the Eve of Epiphany are used at Evening Pray*	

		If Epiphany is celebrated on Wednesday 6 January:	
Saturday	2 January	Isaiah 66.6–14	Matthew 12.46–50
Sunday	3 January	Second Sunday of Christmas	
Monday	4 January	Isaiah 63.7–16	Galatians 3.23—4.7
Tuesday	5 January	At Evening Prayer the readings for the Eve of the Epiphany are used. At other services, the following readings are used:	
		Isaiah 12	2 Corinthians 2.12–end
Wednesday	6 January	The Epiphany – see p. 17	
Thursday	7 January	Genesis 25.19–end	Ephesians 1.1–6
Friday	8 January	Joel 2.28–end	Ephesians 1.7–14
Saturday	9 January	At Evening Prayer the readings for the Eve of the Baptism of Christ are used. At other services, the following readings are used:	
		Proverbs 8.12–21	Ephesians 1.15–end

		If, for pastoral reasons, Epiphany is celebrated on Sunday 3 January:	
Saturday	2 January	At Evening Prayer the readings for the Eve of the Epiphany are used. At other services, the following readings are used:	
		Isaiah 66.6–14	Matthew 12.46–50
Sunday	3 January	The Epiphany – see p. 16	
Monday	4 January	Deuteronomy 6.4–15	John 10.31–end
Tuesday	5 January	Isaiah 63.7–16	Galatians 3.23—4.7
Wednesday	6 January	Isaiah 12	2 Corinthians 2.12–end
Thursday	7 January	Genesis 25.19–end	Ephesians 1.1–6
Friday	8 January	Joel 2.28–end	Ephesians 1.7–14
Saturday	9 January	At Evening Prayer the readings for the Eve of the Baptism of Christ are used. At other services, the following readings are used:	
		Proverbs 8.12–21	Ephesians 1.15–end

Monday	11 January	Isaiah 41.14–20	John 1.29–34
Tuesday	12 January	Exodus 17.1–7	Acts 8.26–end
Wednesday	13 January	Exodus 15.1–19	Colossians 2.8–15
Thursday	14 January	Zechariah 6.9–15	1 Peter 2.4–10
Friday	15 January	Isaiah 51.7–16	Galatians 6.14–18
Saturday	16 January	Leviticus 16.11–22	Hebrews 10.19–25

Monday	18 January	1 Kings 17.8–16	Mark 8.1–10
Tuesday	19 January	1 Kings 19.1–9a	Mark 1.9–15
Wednesday	20 January	1 Kings 19.9b–18	Mark 9.2–13
Thursday	21 January	Leviticus 11.1–8, 13–19, 41–45	Acts 10.9–16
Friday	22 January	Isaiah 49.8–13	Acts 10.34–43
Saturday	23 January	Genesis 35.1–15	Acts 10.44–end

Monday	25 January	Conversion of Paul – see p. 20	
Tuesday	26 January	Ezekiel 20.39–44	John 17.20–end
Wednesday	27 January	Nehemiah 2.1–10	Romans 12.1–8
Thursday	28 January	Deuteronomy 26.16–end	Romans 14.1– 9
Friday	29 January	Leviticus 19.9–28	Romans 15.1–7
Saturday	30 January	Jeremiah 33.1–11	1 Peter 5.5b–end
		If, for pastoral reasons, Presentation of Christ is celebrated on Sunday 31 January the readings for the Eve of the Presentation are used at Evening Prayer.	

Monday	1 February	Jonah 3	2 Corinthians 5.11–21
Tuesday	2 February	Presentation of Christ – see p. 22	
		or, if, for pastoral reasons, Presentation of Christ is celebrated on Sunday 31 January:	
		Proverbs 4.10–end	Matthew 5.13–20
Wednesday	3 February	Isaiah 61.1–9	Luke 7.18–30
Thursday	4 February	Isaiah 52.1–12	Matthew 10.1–15
Friday	5 February	Isaiah 56.1–8	Matthew 28.16–end
Saturday	6 February	Habakkuk 2.1–4	Revelation 14.1–7

Monday	8 February	2 Kings 2.13–22	3 John
Tuesday	9 February	Judges 14.5–17	Revelation 10.4–11
Wednesday	10 February	Ash Wednesday – see p. 24	
Thursday	11 February	Genesis 2.7–end	Hebrews 2.5–end
Friday	12 February	Genesis 4.1–12	Hebrews 4.12–end
Saturday	13 February	2 Kings 22.11–end	Hebrews 5.1–10

14 February – Lent 1

Monday	15 February	Genesis 6.11–end, 7.11–16	Luke 4.14–21
Tuesday	16 February	Deuteronomy 31.7–13	1 John 3.1–10
Wednesday	17 February	Genesis 11.1–9	Matthew 24.15–28
Thursday	18 February	Genesis 13.1–13	1 Peter 2.13–end
Friday	19 February	Genesis 21.1–8	Luke 9.18–27
Saturday	20 February	Genesis 32.22–32	2 Peter 1.10–end

21 February – Lent 2

Monday	22 February	1 Chronicles 21.1–17	1 John 2.1–8
Tuesday	23 February	Zechariah 3	2 Peter 2.1–10a
Wednesday	24 February	Job 1.1–22	Luke 21.34—22.6
Thursday	25 February	2 Chronicles 29.1–11	Mark 11.15–19
Friday	26 February	Exodus 19.1–9a	1 Peter 1.1–9
Saturday	27 February	Exodus 19.9b–19	Acts 7.44–50

28 February – Lent 3

Monday	29 February	Joshua 4.1–13	Luke 9.1–11
Tuesday	1 March	Exodus 15.22–27	Hebrews 10.32–end
Wednesday	2 March	Genesis 9.8–17	1 Peter 3.18–end
Thursday	3 March	Daniel 12.5–end	Mark 13.21–end
Friday	4 March	Numbers 20.1–13	1 Corinthians 10.23–end
Saturday	5 March	Isaiah 43.14–end	Hebrews 3.1–15

6 March – Lent 4

Monday	7 March	2 Kings 24.18—25.7	1 Corinthians 15.20–34
Tuesday	8 March	Jeremiah 13.12–19	Acts 13.26–35
Wednesday	9 March	Jeremiah 13.20–27	1 Peter 1.17—2.3
Thursday	10 March	Jeremiah 22.11–19	Luke 11.37–52
Friday	11 March	Jeremiah 17.1–14	Luke 6.17–26
Saturday	12 March	Ezra 1	2 Corinthians 1.12–19

13 March – Lent 5

Monday	14 March	Joel 2.12–17	2 John
Tuesday	15 March	Isaiah 58.1–14	Mark 10.32–45
Wednesday	16 March	Job 36.1–12	John 14.1–14
Thursday	17 March	Jeremiah 9.17–22	Luke 13.31–35
Friday	18 March	Lamentations 5.1–3,19–22 or 1st EP of Joseph of Nazareth	John 12.20–26
Saturday	19 March	Joseph of Nazareth – see p. 29	

From the Monday of Holy Week until Easter Eve the seasonal lectionary is used: see pp. 30–31.

27 March – Easter

Monday	28 March	Isaiah 54.1–14	Romans 1.1–7
Tuesday	29 March	Isaiah 51.1–11	John 5.19–29
Wednesday	30 March	Isaiah 26.1–19	John 20.1–10
Thursday	31 March	Isaiah 43.14–21	Revelation 1.4–end
Friday	1 April	Isaiah 42.10–17	1 Thessalonians 5.1–11
Saturday	2 April	Job 14.1–14	John 21.1–14

3 April – Easter 2

Monday	4 April	Annunciation of Our Lord to the Blessed Virgin Mary transferred – see p. 33	
Tuesday	5 April	Proverbs 8.1–11	Acts 16.6–15
Wednesday	6 April	Hosea 5.15—6.6	1 Corinthians 15.1–11
Thursday	7 April	Jonah 2	Mark 4.35–end
Friday	8 April	Genesis 6.9–end	1 Peter 3.8–end
Saturday	9 April	1 Samuel 2.1–8	Matthew 28.8–15

Monday	11 April	Exodus 24.1–11	Revelation 5
Tuesday	12 April	Leviticus 19.9–18, 32–end	Matthew 5.38–end
Wednesday	13 April	Genesis 3.8–21	1 Corinthians 15.12–28
Thursday	14 April	Isaiah 33.13–22	Mark 6.47–end
Friday	15 April	Nehemiah 9.6–17	Romans 5.12–end
Saturday	16 April	Isaiah 61.10—62.5	Luke 24.1–12

Monday	18 April	Jeremiah 31.10–17	Revelation 7.9–end
Tuesday	19 April	Job 31.13–23	Matthew 7.1–12
Wednesday	20 April	Genesis 2.4b–9	1 Corinthians 15.35–49
Thursday	21 April	Proverbs 28.3–end	Mark 10.17–31
Friday	22 April	Ecclesiastes 12.1–8	Romans 6.1–11
		or 1st EP of George, Martyr, Patron of England	
Saturday	23 April	George, Martyr, Patron of England – see p. 35	

Monday	25 April	Mark the Evangelist – see p. 36	
Tuesday	26 April	Deuteronomy 8.1–10	Matthew 6.19–end
Wednesday	27 April	Hosea 13.4–14	1 Corinthians 15.50–end
Thursday	28 April	Exodus 3.1–15	Mark 12.18–27
Friday	29 April	Ezekiel 36.33–end	Romans 8.1–11
Saturday	30 April	Isaiah 38.9–20	Luke 24.33–end

Monday	2 May	Philip and James, Apostles transferred – see p. 37	
Tuesday	3 May	Isaiah 32.12–end	Romans 5.1–11
Wednesday	4 May	At Evening Prayer the readings for the Eve of Ascension Day are used. At other services, the following readings are used:	
		Isaiah 43.1–13	Titus 2.11—3.8
Thursday	5 May	Ascension Day – see p. 38	
Friday	6 May	Exodus 35.30—36.1	Galatians 5.13–end
Saturday	7 May	Numbers 11.16–17, 24–29	1 Corinthians 2

Monday	9 May	Numbers 27.15–end	1 Corinthians 3
Tuesday	10 May	1 Samuel 10.1–10	1 Corinthians 12.1–13
Wednesday	11 May	1 Kings 19.1–18	Matthew 3.13–end
Thursday	12 May	Ezekiel 11.14–20	Matthew 9.35—10.20
Friday	13 May	Ezekiel 36.22–28	Matthew 12.22–32
Saturday	14 May	Matthias the Apostle – see p. 39. At Evening Prayer the readings for the Eve of Pentecost are used. At other services, the following readings are used if Matthias is celebrated on Monday 25 February:	
		Micah 3.1–8	Ephesians 6.10–20

Monday	16 May	Genesis 12.1–9	Romans 4.13–end
Tuesday	17 May	Genesis 13.1–12	Romans 12.9–end
Wednesday	18 May	Genesis 15	Romans 4.1–8
Thursday	19 May	Genesis 22.1–18	Hebrews 11.8–19
Friday	20 May	Isaiah 51.1–8	John 8.48–end
Saturday	21 May	At Evening Prayer the readings for the Eve of Trinity Sunday are used. At other services, the following readings are used:	
		Ecclesiasticus 44.19–23	James 2.14–26
		or Joshua 2.1–15	

Monday	23 May	Exodus 2.1–10	Hebrews 11.23–31
Tuesday	24 May	Exodus 2.11–end	Acts 7.17–29
Wednesday	25 May	Exodus 3.1–12	Acts 7.30–38
		or 1st EP of Corpus Christi	
Thursday	26 May	Day of Thanksgiving for the Institution of the Holy Communion (Corpus Christi) – see p. 41	
		or, where Corpus Christi is celebrated as a Lesser Festival:	
		Exodus 6.1–13	John 9.24–38
Friday	27 May	Exodus 34.1–10	Mark 7.1–13
Saturday	28 May	Exodus 34.27–end	2 Corinthians 3.7–end

Monday	30 May	Genesis 37.1–11	Romans 11.9–21
		or 1st EP of the Visit of the Blessed Virgin Mary to Elizabeth	
Tuesday	31 May	Visit of the Blessed Virgin Mary to Elizabeth – see p. 42	
Wednesday	1 June	Genesis 42.17–end	Matthew 18.1–14
Thursday	2 June	Genesis 45.1–15	Acts 7.9–16
Friday	3 June	Genesis 47.1–12	1 Thessalonians 5.12–end
Saturday	4 June	Genesis 50.4–21	Luke 15.11–end

Monday	6 June	Isaiah 32	James 3.13–end
Tuesday	7 June	Proverbs 3.1–18	Matthew 5.1–12
Wednesday	8 June	Judges 6.1–16	Matthew 5.13–24
Thursday	9 June	Jeremiah 6.9–15	1 Timothy 2.1–6
Friday	10 June	1 Samuel 16.14–end	John 14.15–end
		or 1st EP of Barnabas the Apostle	
Saturday	11 June	Barnabas the Apostle – see p. 43	

Monday	13 June	Exodus 13.13b–end	Luke 15.1–10
Tuesday	14 June	Proverbs 1.20–end	James 5.13–end
Wednesday	15 June	Isaiah 5.8–24	James 1.17–25
Thursday	16 June	Isaiah 57.14–end	John 13.1–17
Friday	17 June	Jeremiah 15.15–end	Luke 16.19–31
Saturday	18 June	Isaiah 25.1–9	Acts 2.22–33

Monday	20 June	Exodus 20.1–17	Matthew 6.1–15
Tuesday	21 June	Proverbs 6.6–19	Luke 4.1–14
Wednesday	22 June	Isaiah 24.1–15	1 Corinthians 6.1–11
Thursday	23 June	Job 7	Matthew 7.21–29
		or 1st EP of Birth of John the Baptist	
Friday	24 June	Birth of John the Baptist – see p. 45	
Saturday	25 June	Job 28	Hebrews 11.32—12.2

Monday	27 June	Exodus 32.1–14	Colossians 3.1–11
Tuesday	28 June	Proverbs 9.1–12	2 Thessalonians 2.13—3.1
		or 1st EP of Peter and Paul, Apostles (or Peter the Apostle)	
Wednesday	29 June	Peter and Paul, Apostles (or Peter the Apostle) – see p. 46	
Thursday	30 June	Jeremiah 8.18—9.6	John 13.21–35
Friday	1 July	2 Samuel 5.1–12	Matthew 27.45–56
Saturday	2 July	Hosea 11.1–11	Matthew 28.1–7
		or 1st EP of Thomas the Apostle	

Monday	4 July	Exodus 40.1–16	Luke 14.15–24
		or Thomas the Apostle transferred – see p. 47	
Tuesday	5 July	Proverbs 11.1–12	Mark 12.38–44
Wednesday	6 July	Isaiah 33.2–10	Philippians 1.1–11
Thursday	7 July	Job 38	Luke 18.1–14
Friday	8 July	Job 42.1–6	John 3.1–15
Saturday	9 July	Ecclesiastes 9.1–11	Hebrews 1.1–9

	10 July – Trinity 7		
Monday	11 July	Numbers 23.1–12	1 Corinthians 1.10–17
Tuesday	12 July	Proverbs 12.1–12	Galatians 3.1–14
Wednesday	13 July	Isaiah 49.8–13	2 Corinthians 8.1–11
Thursday	14 July	Hosea 14	John 15.1–17
Friday	15 July	2 Samuel 18.18–end	Matthew 27.57–66
Saturday	16 July	Isaiah 55.1–7	Mark 16.1–8
	17 July – Trinity 8		
Monday	18 July	Joel 3.16–21	Mark 4.21–34
Tuesday	19 July	Proverbs 12.13–end	John 1.43–51
Wednesday	20 July	Isaiah 55.8–end	2 Timothy 2.8–19
Thursday	21 July	Isaiah 38.1–8	Mark 5.21–43
		or 1st EP of Mary Magdalene	
Friday	22 July	Mary Magdalene – see p. 50	
Saturday	23 July	Ecclesiastes 5.10–19	1 Timothy 6.6–16
	24 July – Trinity 9		
Monday	25 July	James the Apostle – see p. 51	
Tuesday	26 July	Proverbs 15.1–11	Galatians 2.15–end
Wednesday	27 July	Isaiah 49.1–7	1 John 1
Thursday	28 July	Proverbs 27.1–12	John 15.12–27
Friday	29 July	Isaiah 59.8–end	Mark 15.6–20
Saturday	30 July	Zechariah 7.8–8.8	Luke 20.27–40
	31 July – Trinity 10		
Monday	1 August	Judges 13.1–23	Luke 10.38–42
Tuesday	2 August	Proverbs 15.15–end	Matthew 15.21–28
Wednesday	3 August	Isaiah 45.1–7	Ephesians 4.1–16
Thursday	4 August	Jeremiah 16.1–15	Luke 12.35–48
Friday	5 August	Jeremiah 18.1–11	Hebrews 1.1–9
		or 1st EP of Transfiguration of Our Lord	
Saturday	6 August	Transfiguration of Our Lord – see p. 52	
	7 August – Trinity 11		
Monday	8 August	Ruth 2.1–13	Luke 10.25–37
Tuesday	9 August	Proverbs 16.1–11	Philippians 3.4b–end
Wednesday	10 August	Deuteronomy 11.1–21	2 Corinthians 9.6–end
Thursday	11 August	Ecclesiasticus 2	John 16.1–15
		or Ecclesiastes 2.12–25	
Friday	12 August	Obadiah 1–10	John 19.1–16
Saturday	13 August	2 Kings 2.11–14	Luke 24.36–end
	14 August – Trinity 12		
Monday	15 August	The Blessed Virgin Mary – see p. 54	
Tuesday	16 August	Proverbs 17.1–15	Luke 7.1–17
Wednesday	17 August	Jeremiah 5.20–end	2 Peter 3.8–end
Thursday	18 August	Daniel 2.1–23	Luke 10.1–20
Friday	19 August	Daniel 3.1–28	Revelation 15
Saturday	20 August	Daniel 6	Philippians 2.14–24
	21 August – Trinity 13		
Monday	22 August	2 Samuel 7.4–17	2 Corinthians 5.1–10
Tuesday	23 August	Proverbs 18.10–21	Romans 14.10–end
		or 1st EP of Bartholomew the Apostle	
Wednesday	24 August	Bartholomew the Apostle – see p. 55	
Thursday	25 August	Isaiah 49.14–end	John 16.16–24
Friday	26 August	Job 9.1–24	Mark 15.21–32
Saturday	27 August	Exodus 19.1–9	John 20.11–18

Monday	17 October	I Kings 8.22–30	John 12.12–19
		or 1st EP of Luke the Evangelist	
Tuesday	18 October	Luke the Evangelist – see p. 63	
Wednesday	19 October	Hosea 14.1–7	2 Timothy 4.1–8
Thursday	20 October	Isaiah 49.1–7	John 19.16–25a
Friday	21 October	Proverbs 24.3–22	John 8.1–11
Saturday	22 October	Ecclesiasticus 7.8–17, 32–end	2 Timothy 1.1–14
		or Deuteronomy 6.16–25	

Monday	24 October	Isaiah 42.14–21	Luke 1.5–25
Tuesday	25 October	I Samuel 4.12–end	Luke 1.57–80
Wednesday	26 October	Baruch 5 or Haggai 1.1–11	Mark 1.1–11
Thursday	27 October	Isaiah 35	Matthew 11.2–19
		or 1st EP of Simon and Jude, Apostles	
Friday	28 October	Simon and Jude, Apostles – see p. 64	
Saturday	29 October	Isaiah 43.15–21	Acts 19.1–10
		or 1st EP of All Saints' Day if All Saints' Day is celebrated on 30 October	

Monday	31 October	Esther 3.1–11, 4.7–17	Matthew 18.1–10
		or 1st EP of All Saints' Day	
Tuesday	I November	All Saints' Day – see p. 66	
		or, if All Saints' Day is celebrated on Sunday 30 October only, the following readings are used:	
		Ezekiel 18.21–end	Matthew 18.12–20
Wednesday	2 November	Proverbs 3.27–end	Matthew 18.21–end
Thursday	3 November	Exodus 23.1–9	Matthew 19.1–15
Friday	4 November	Proverbs 3.13–18	Matthew 19.16–end
Saturday	5 November	Deuteronomy 28.1–6	Matthew 20.1–16

Monday	7 November	Isaiah 40.21–end	Romans 11.25–end
Tuesday	8 November	Ezekiel 34.20–end	John 10.1–18
Wednesday	9 November	Leviticus 26.3–13	Titus 2.1–10
Thursday	10 November	Hosea 6.1–6	Matthew 9.9–13
Friday	11 November	Malachi 4	John 4.5–26
Saturday	12 November	Micah 6.6–8	Colossians 3.12–17

Monday	14 November	Micah 7.1–7	Matthew 10.24–39
Tuesday	15 November	Habakkuk 3.1–19a	I Corinthians 4.9–16
Wednesday	16 November	Zechariah 8.1–13	Mark 13.3–8
Thursday	17 November	Zechariah 10.6–end	I Peter 5.1–11
Friday	18 November	Micah 4.1–5	Luke 9.28–36
Saturday	19 November	Exodus 16.1–21	John 6.3–15
		or 1st EP of Christ the King	

Monday	21 November	Jeremiah 30.1–3, 10–17	Romans 12.9–21
Tuesday	22 November	Jeremiah 30.18–24	John 10.22–30
Wednesday	23 November	Jeremiah 31.1–9	Matthew 15.21–31
Thursday	24 November	Jeremiah 31.10–17	Matthew 16.13–end
Friday	25 November	Jeremiah 31.31–37	Hebrews 10.11–18
Saturday	26 November	Isaiah 51.17—52.2	Ephesians 5.1–20

¶ Collects and Post Communions

All the contemporary language Collects and Post Communions, including the Additional Collects, may be found in *Common Worship: Collects and Post Communions* (Church House Publishing: London, 2004). The Additional Collects are also published separately.

The contemporary language Collects and Post Communions all appear in *Times and Seaso President's Edition for Holy Communion*. Apart from the Additional Collects, they appear in th other Common Worship volumes as follows:

¶ President's edition: all Collects and Post Communions;
¶ *Daily Prayer*: all Collects;
¶ main volume: Collects and Post Communions for Sundays, Principal Feasts and Holy D and Festivals;
¶ *Festivals*: Collects and Post Communions for Festivals, Lesser Festivals, Common of the Saints and Special Occasions.

The traditional-language Collects and Post Communions all appear in the president's editi They appear in other publications as follows:

¶ main volume: Collects and Post Communions for Sundays, Principal Feasts and Holy D and Festivals;
¶ separate booklet: Collects and Post Communions for Lesser Festivals, Common of the Saints and Special Occasions.

¶ Lectionary for Dedication Festival

If date not known, observe on the first Sunday in October or Last Sunday after Trinity.

Evening Prayer on the Eve
Psalm 24
2 Chronicles 7.11–16
John 4.19–29

Dedication Festival
Gold or White

	Principal Service	3rd Service	2nd Service	Psalmo
Year A	I Kings 8.22–30 *or* Revelation 21.9–14 Psalm 122 Hebrews 12.18–24 Matthew 21.12–16	Haggai 2.6–9 Hebrews 10.19–25	Jeremiah 7.1–11 I Corinthians 3.9–17 *HC* Luke 19.1–10	*MP* 48, I *EP* 132
Year B	Genesis 28.11–18 *or* Revelation 21.9–14 Psalm 122 I Peter 2.1–10 John 10.22–29	Haggai 2.6–9 Hebrews 10.19–25	Jeremiah 7.1–11 Luke 19.1–10	*MP* 48, I *EP* 132
Year C	I Chronicles 29.6–19 Psalm 122 Ephesians 2.19–22 John 2.13–22	Haggai 2.6–9 Hebrews 10.19–25	Jeremiah 7.1–11 Luke 19.1–10	*MP* 48, I *EP* 132

The Blessed Virgin Mary

Genesis 3.8–15, 20; Isaiah 7.10–14; Micah 5.1–4
Psalms 45.10–17; 113; 131
Acts 1.12–14; Romans 8.18–30; Galatians 4.4–7
Luke 1.26–38; *or* 1.39–47; John 19.25–27

Martyrs

2 Chronicles 24.17–21; Isaiah 43.1–7; Jeremiah 11.18–20; Wisdom 4.10–15
Psalms 3; 11; 31.1–5; 44.18–24; 126
Romans 8.35–end; 2 Corinthians 4.7–15; 2 Timothy 2.3–7 [8–13]; Hebrews 11.32–end;
    1 Peter 4.12–end; Revelation 12.10–12a
Matthew 10.16–22; *or* 10.28–39; *or* 16.24–26; John 12.24–26; *or* 15.18–21

Agnes (21 Jan): *also* Revelation 7.13–end
Alban (22 June): *especially* 2 Timothy 2.3–13; John 12.24–26
Alphege (19 Apr): *also* Hebrews 5.1–4
Boniface (5 June): *also* Acts 20.24–28
Charles (30 Jan): *also* Ecclesiasticus 2.12–end; 1 Timothy 6.12–16
Clement (23 Nov): *also* Philippians 3.17—4.3; Matthew 16.13–19
Cyprian (15 Sept): *especially* 1 Peter 4.12–end; *also* Matthew 18.18–22
Edmund (20 Nov): *also* Proverbs 20.28; 21.1–4, 7
Ignatius (17 Oct): *also* Philippians 3.7–12; John 6.52–58
James Hannington (29 Oct): *especially* Matthew 10.28–39
Janani Luwum (17 Feb): *also* Ecclesiasticus 4.20–28; John 12.24–26
John Coleridge Patteson (20 Sept): *especially* 2 Chronicles 24.17–21; *also* Acts 7.55–end
Justin (1 June): *especially* John 15.18–21; *also* 1 Maccabees 2.15–22; 1 Corinthians 1.18–25
Laurence (10 Aug): *also* 2 Corinthians 9.6–10
Lucy (13 Dec): *also* Wisdom 3.1–7; 2 Corinthians 4.6–15
Oswald (5 Aug): *especially* 1 Peter 4.12–end; John 16.29–end
Perpetua, Felicity and comps (7 Mar): *especially* Revelation 12.10–12a; *also* Wisdom 3.1–7
Polycarp (23 Feb): *also* Revelation 2.8–11
Thomas Becket (29 Dec *or* 7 Jul): *especially* Matthew 10.28–33; *also* Ecclesiasticus 51.1–8
William Tyndale (6 Oct): *also* Proverbs 8.4–11; 2 Timothy 3.12–end

Teachers of the Faith and Spiritual Writers

1 Kings 3.[6–10] 11–14; Proverbs 4.1–9; Wisdom 7.7–10, 15–16; Ecclesiasticus 39.1–10
Psalms 19.7–10; 34.11–17; 37.31–35; 119.89–96; 119.97–104
1 Corinthians 1.18–25; *or* 2.1–10; *or* 2.9–end; Ephesians 3.8–12; 2 Timothy 4.1–8;
    Titus 2.1–8
Matthew 5.13–19; *or* 13.52–end; *or* 23.8–12; Mark 4.1–9; John 16.12–15

Ambrose (7 Dec): *also* Isaiah 41.9b–13; Luke 22.24–30
Anselm (21 Apr): *also* Wisdom 9.13–end; Romans 5.8–11
Athanasius (2 May): *also* Ecclesiasticus 4.20–28; *also* Matthew 10.24–27
Augustine of Hippo (28 Aug): *especially* Ecclesiasticus 39.1–10; *also* Romans 13.11–13
Basil and Gregory (2 Jan): *especially* 2 Timothy 4.1–8; Matthew 5.13–19
Bernard (20 Aug): *especially* Revelation 19.5–9
Catherine of Siena (29 Apr): *also* Proverbs 8.1, 6–11; John 17.12–end
Francis de Sales (24 Jan): *also* Proverbs 3.13–18; John 3.17–21
Gregory the Great (3 Sept): *also* 1 Thessalonians 2.3–8
Gregory of Nyssa and Macrina (19 July): *especially* 1 Corinthians 2.9–13;
    also Wisdom 9.13–17
Hilary (13 Jan): *also* 1 John 2.18–25; John 8.25–32
Irenaeus (28 June): *also* 2 Peter 1.16–end
Jeremy Taylor (13 Aug); *also* Titus 2.7–8, 11–14
John Bunyan (30 Aug): *also* Hebrews 12.1–2; Luke 21.21, 34–36
John Chrysostom (13 Sept): *especially* Matthew 5.13–19; *also* Jeremiah 1.4–10
John of the Cross (14 Dec): *especially* 1 Corinthians 2.1–10; *also* John 14.18–23
Leo (10 Nov): *also* 1 Peter 5.1–11
Richard Hooker (3 Nov): *especially* John 16.12–15; *also* Ecclesiasticus 44.10–15
Teresa of Avila (15 Oct): *also* Romans 8.22–27
Thomas Aquinas (28 Jan): *especially* Wisdom 7.7–10, 15–16; 1 Corinthians 2.9–end;
    John 16.12–15
William Law (10 Apr): *especially* 1 Corinthians 2.9–end; *also* Matthew 17.1–9

Bishops and Other Pastors

1 Samuel 16.1, 6–13; Isaiah 6.1–8; Jeremiah 1.4–10; Ezekiel 3.16–21; Malachi 2.5–7
Psalms 1; 15; 16.5–end; 96; 110
Acts 20.28–35; 1 Corinthians 4.1–5; 2 Corinthians 4.1–10 [or 1–2, 5–7];
     or 5.14–20; 1 Peter 5.1–4
Matthew 11.25–end; or 24.42–46; John 10.11–16; or 15.9–17; or 21.15–17

Augustine of Canterbury (26 May): also 1 Thessalonians 2.2b–8; Matthew 13.31–33
Charles Simeon (13 Nov): especially Malachi 2.5–7; also Colossians 1.3–8; Luke 8.4–8
David (1 Mar): also 2 Samuel 23.1–4; Psalm 89.19–22, 24
Dunstan (19 May): especially Matthew 24.42–46; also Exodus 31.1–5
Edward King (8 Mar): also Hebrews 13.1–8
George Herbert (27 Feb): especially Malachi 2.5–7; Matthew 11.25–end;
     also Revelation 19.5–9
Hugh (17 Nov); also 1 Timothy 6.11–16
John Keble (14 July): also Lamentations 3.19–26; Matthew 5.1–8
John and Charles Wesley (24 May): also Ephesians 5.15–20
Lancelot Andrewes (25 Sept): especially Isaiah 6.1–8
Martin of Tours (11 Nov): also 1 Thessalonians 5.1–11; Matthew 25.34–40
Nicholas (6 Dec): also Isaiah 61.1–3; 1 Timothy 6.6–11; Mark 10.13–16
Richard (16 June): also John 21.15–19
Swithun (15 July): also James 5.7–11, 13–18
Thomas Ken (8 June): especially 2 Corinthians 4.1–10 [or 1–2, 5–7]; Matthew 24.42–46
Wulfstan (19 Jan): especially Matthew 24.42–46

Members of Religious Communities

1 Kings 19.9–18; Proverbs 10.27–end; Song of Solomon 8.6–7; Isaiah 61.10—62.5;
    Hosea 2.14–15, 19–20
Psalms 34.1–8; 112.1–9; 119.57–64; 123; 131
Acts 4.32–35; 2 Corinthians 10.17—11.2; Philippians 3.7–14; 1 John 2.15–17;
    Revelation 19.1, 5–9
Matthew 11.25–end; *or* 19.3–12; *or* 19.23–end; Luke 9.57–end; *or* 12.32–37

Aelred (12 Jan): *also* Ecclesiasticus 15.1–6
Alcuin (20 May): *also* Colossians 3.12–16; John 4.19–24
Antony (17 Jan): *especially* Philippians 3.7–14, *also* Matthew 19.16–26
Bede (25 May): *also* Ecclesiasticus 39.1–10
Benedict (11 July): *also* 1 Corinthians 3.10–11; Luke 18.18–22
Clare (11 Aug): *especially* Song of Solomon 8.6–7
Dominic (8 Aug): *also* Ecclesiasticus 39.1–10
Etheldreda (23 June): *also* Matthew 25.1–13
Francis of Assisi (4 Oct): *also* Galatians 6.14–end; Luke 12.22–34
Hilda (19 Nov): *especially* Isaiah 61.10—62.5
Hildegard (17 Sept): *also* 1 Corinthians 2.9–13; Luke 10.21–24
Julian of Norwich (8 May): *also* 1 Corinthians 13.8–end; Matthew 5.13–16
Vincent de Paul (27 Sept): *also* 1 Corinthians 1.25–end; Matthew 25.34–40

Missionaries

Isaiah 52.7–10; *or* 61.1–3a; Ezekiel 34.11–16; Jonah 3.1–5
Psalms 67; *or* 87; *or* 97; *or* 100; *or* 117
Acts 2.14, 22–36; *or* 13.46–49; *or* 16.6–10; *or* 26.19–23; Romans 15.17–21;
    2 Corinthians 5.11—6.2
Matthew 9.35–end; *or* 28.16–end; Mark 16.15–20; Luke 5.1–11; *or* 10.1–9

Aidan (31 Aug): *also* 1 Corinthians 9.16–19
Anskar (3 Feb): *especially* Isaiah 52.7–10; *also* Romans 10.11–15
Chad (2 Mar *or* 26 Oct): *also* 1 Timothy 6.11b–16
Columba (9 June): *also* Titus 2.11–end
Cuthbert (20 Mar *or* 4 Sept): *especially* Ezekiel 34.11–16; *also* Matthew 18.12–14
Cyril and Methodius (14 Feb): *especially* Isaiah 52.7–10; *also* Romans 10.11–15
Henry Martyn (19 Oct): *especially* Mark 16.15–end; *also* Isaiah 55.6–11
Ninian (16 Sept): *especially* Acts 13.46–49; Mark 16.15–end
Patrick (17 Mar): *also* Psalm 91.1–4, 13–end; Luke 10.1–12, 17–20
Paulinus (10 Oct); *especially* Matthew 28.16–end
Wilfrid (12 Oct): *especially* Luke 5.1–11; *also* 1 Corinthians 1.18–25
Willibrord (7 Nov): *especially* Isaiah 52.7–10; Matthew 28.16–end

Any Saint

General

Genesis 12.1–4; Proverbs 8.1–11; Micah 6.6–8; Ecclesiasticus 2.7–13 [14–end]
Psalms 32; 33.1–5; 119.1–8; 139.1–4 [5–12]; 145.8–14
Ephesians 3.14–19; or 6.11–18; Hebrews 13.7–8, 15–16; James 2.14–17;
    1 John 4.7–16; Revelation 21.[1–4] 5–7
Matthew 19.16–21; or 25.1–13; or 25.14–30; John 15.1–8; or 17.20–end

Christian rulers

1 Samuel 16.1–13a; 1 Kings 3.3–14
Psalms 72.1–7; 99
1 Timothy 2.1–6
Mark 10.42–45; Luke 14.27–33

Alfred the Great (26 Oct): also 2 Samuel 23.1–5; John 18.33–37
Edward the Confessor (13 Oct): also 2 Samuel 23.1–5; 1 John 4.13–16
Margaret of Scotland (16 Nov): also Proverbs 31.10–12, 20, 26–end;
    1 Corinthians 12.13—13.3; Matthew 25.34–end

Those working for the poor and underprivileged

Isaiah 58.6–11
Psalms 82; 146.5–10
Hebrews 13.1–3; 1 John 3.14–18
Matthew 5.1–12; or 25.31–end

Elizabeth of Hungary (18 Nov): especially Matthew 25.31–end; also Proverbs 31.10–end
Josephine Butler (30 May): especially Isaiah 58.6–11; also 1 John 3.18–23; Matthew 9.10–13
William Wilberforce, Olaudah Equiano and Thomas Clarkson (30 July): also Job 31.16–23;
    Galatians 3.26–end, 4.6–7; Luke 4.16–21

Men and women of learning

Proverbs 8.22–31; Ecclesiasticus 44.1–15
Psalms 36.5–10; 49.1–4
Philippians 4.7–8
Matthew 13.44–46, 52; John 7.14–18

Those whose holiness was revealed in marriage and family life

Proverbs 31.10–13, 19–20, 30–end; Tobit 8.4–7
Psalms 127; 128
1 Peter 3.1–9
Mark 3.31–end; Luke 10.38–end

Mary Sumner (9 Aug): also Hebrews 13.1–5
Monica (27 Aug): also Ecclesiasticus 26.1–3, 13–16

The Guidance of the Holy Spirit

Proverbs 24.3–7; Isaiah 30.15–21; Wisdom 9.13–17
Psalms 25.1–9; 104.26–33; 143.8–10
Acts 15.23–29; Romans 8:22–27; 1 Corinthians 12.4–13
Luke 14.27–33; John 14.23–26; *or* 16.13–15

Rogation Days
(2–4 May in 2016)

Deuteronomy 8.1–10; 1 Kings 8.35–40; Job 28.1–11
Psalms 104.21–30; 107.1–9; 121
Philippians 4.4–7; 2 Thessalonians 3.6–13; 1 John 5.12–15
Matthew 6.1–15; Mark 11.22–24; Luke 11.5–13

Harvest Thanksgiving

Year A	Year B	Year C
Deuteronomy 8.7–18 *or* 28.1–14	Joel 2.21–27	Deuteronomy 26.1–⏏
Psalm 65	Psalm 126	Psalm 100
2 Corinthians 9.6–end	1 Timothy 2.1–7 *or* 6.6–10	Philippians 4.4–9
Luke 12.16–30 *or* 17.11–19	Matthew 6.25–33	*or* Revelation 14.14–
		John 6.25–35

Mission and Evangelism

Isaiah 49.1–6; *or* 52.7–10; Micah 4.1–5
Psalms 2; 46; 67
Acts 17.10–end; 2 Corinthians 5.14—6.2; Ephesians 2.13–end
Matthew 5.13–16; *or* 28.16–end; John 17.20–end

The Unity of the Church

Jeremiah 33.6–9a; Ezekiel 36.23–28; Zephaniah 3.16–end
Psalms 100; 122; 133
Ephesians 4.1–6; Colossians 3.9–17; 1 John 4.9–15
Matthew 18.19–22; John 11.45–52; *or* 17.11b–23

The Peace of the World

Isaiah 9.1–6; *or* 57.15–19; Micah 4.1–5
Psalms 40.14–17; 72.1–7; 85.8–13
Philippians 4.6–9; 1 Timothy 2.1–6; James 3.13–18
Matthew 5.43–end; John 14.23–29; *or* 15.9–17

Social Justice and Responsibility

Isaiah 32.15–end; Amos 5.21–24; *or* 8.4–7; Acts 5.1–11
Psalms 31.21–24; 85.1–7; 146.5–10
Colossians 3.12–15; James 2.1–4
Matthew 5.1–12; *or* 25.31–end; Luke 16.19–end

Ministry, including Ember Days
(See page 7)

Numbers 11.16–17, 24–29; *or* 27.15–end; 1 Samuel 16.1–13a; Isaiah 6.1–8;
    or 61.1–3; Jeremiah 1.4–10
Psalms 40.8–13; 84.8–12; 89.19–25; 101.1–5, 7; 122
Acts 20.28–35; 1 Corinthians 3.3–11; Ephesians 4.4–16; Philippians 3.7–14
Luke 4.16–21; *or* 12.35–43; *or* 22.24–27; John 4.31–38; *or* 15.5–17

In Time of Trouble

Genesis 9.8–17; Job 1.13–end; Isaiah 38.6–11
Psalms 86.1–7; 107.4–15; 142.1–7
Romans 3.21–26; Romans 8.18–25; 2 Corinthians 8.1–5, 9
Mark 4.35–end; Luke 12.1–7; John 16.31–end

For the Sovereign

Joshua 1.1–9; Proverbs 8.1–16
Psalms 20; 101; 121
Romans 13.1–10; Revelation 21.22—22.4
Matthew 22.16–22; Luke 22.24–30

The anniversary of HM The Queen's accession is 6 February.

The following provision may be used for a monthly cycle of psalmody in place of the psalms provid
in the tables in this booklet. It is based on the provision in The Book of Common Prayer.

	Morning Prayer	**Evening Prayer**
1	1—5	6—8
2	9—11	12—14
3	15—17	18
4	19—21	22—23
5	24—26	27—29
6	30—31	32—34
7	35—36	37
8	38—40	41—43
9	44—46	47—49
10	50—52	53—55
11	56—58	59—61
12	62—64	65—67
13	68	69—70
14	71—72	73—74
15	75—77	78
16	79—81	82—85
17	86—88	89
18	90—92	93—94
19	95—97	98—101
20	102—103	104
21	105	106
22	107	108—109
23	110—112	113—115
24	116—118	119.1—32
25	119.33–72	119.73–96
26	119.97–144	119.145–176
27	120—125	126—131
28	132—135	136—138
29	139—140	141—143
30	144—146	147—150

In February the psalms are read only to the 28th or 29th day of the month.

In January, March, May, July, August, October and December, all of which have 31 days, the
same psalms are read on the last day of the month (being an ordinary weekday) which we
read the day before, or else the psalms of the monthly course omitted on one of the Sund
in that month.

Concise Calendar November 2016 – December 2017

Advent 2016 to the eve of Advent 2017: Year A (Daily Eucharistic Lectionary Year 1)

November 2016

Sunday		3bAdv	2bAdv	ChrK	Adv1
Monday		7	14	21	28
Tuesday	AllSS	8	15	22	29
Wednesday	2	9	16	23	30
Thursday	3	10	17	24	
Friday	4	11	18	25	
Saturday	5	12	19	26	

December 2016

Sunday		Adv2	Adv3	Adv4	Chr
Monday		5	12	19	26
Tuesday		6	13	20	27
Wednesday		7	14	21	28
Thursday	1	8	15	22	29
Friday	2	9	16	23	30
Saturday	3	10	17	24	31

January 2017

Sunday	Chr1	Bapt	Ep2	Ep3	Ep4
Monday	2	9	16	23	30
Tuesday	3	10	17	24	31
Wednesday	4	11	18	25	
Thursday	5	12	19	26	
Friday	Epiph	13	20	27	
Saturday	7	14	21	28	

February 2017

Sunday		4bLnt	3bLnt	2bLnt	SbLnt
Monday		6	13	20	27
Tuesday		7	14	21	28
Wednesday	1	8	15	22	
Thursday	Pres	9	16	23	
Friday	3	10	17	24	
Saturday	4	11	18	25	

March 2017

Sunday		Lnt1	Lnt2	Lnt3	Lnt4
Monday		6	13	20	27
Tuesday		7	14	21	28
Wednesday	Ash W	8	15	22	29
Thursday	2	9	16	23	30
Friday	3	10	17	24	31
Saturday	4	11	18	Ann	

April 2017

Sunday		Lnt5	PmS	Est	Est2	Est3
Monday		3	10	17	24	
Tuesday		4	11	18	25	
Wednesday		5	12	19	26	
Thursday		6	13	20	27	
Friday		7	14	21	28	
Saturday	1	8	15	22	29	

May 2017

Sunday		Est4	Est5	Est6	Est7
Monday	1	8	15	22	29
Tuesday	2	9	16	23	30
Wednesday	3	10	17	24	31
Thursday	4	11	18	Ascn	
Friday	5	12	19	26	
Saturday	6	13	20	27	

June 2017

Sunday		Pent	TrS	Tr1	Tr2
Monday		5	12	19	26
Tuesday		6	13	20	27
Wednesday		7	14	21	28
Thursday	1	8	15	22	29
Friday	2	9	16	23	30
Saturday	3	10	17	24	

July 2017

Sunday		Tr3	Tr4	Tr5	Tr6	Tr7
Monday		3	10	17	24	31
Tuesday		4	11	18	25	
Wednesday		5	12	19	26	
Thursday		6	13	20	27	
Friday		7	14	21	28	
Saturday	1	8	15	22	29	

August 2017

Sunday		Tr8	Tr9	Tr10	Tr11
Monday		7	14	21	28
Tuesday	1	8	15	22	29
Wednesday	2	9	16	23	30
Thursday	3	10	17	24	31
Friday	4	11	18	25	
Saturday	5	12	19	26	

September 2017

Sunday		Tr12	Tr13	Tr14	Tr15
Monday		4	11	18	25
Tuesday		5	12	19	26
Wednesday		6	13	20	27
Thursday		7	14	21	28
Friday	1	8	15	22	29
Saturday	2	9	16	23	30

October 2017

Sunday	Tr16	Tr17	Tr18	Tr19	LstTr
Monday	2	9	16	23	30
Tuesday	3	10	17	24	31
Wednesday	4	11	18	25	
Thursday	5	12	19	26	
Friday	6	13	20	27	
Saturday	7	14	21	28	

November 2017

Sunday		4bAdv	3bAdv	2bAdv	ChrK
Monday		6	13	20	27
Tuesday		7	14	21	28
Wednesday	AllSs	8	15	22	29
Thursday	2	9	16	23	30
Friday	3	10	17	24	
Saturday	4	11	18	25	

December 2017

Sunday		Adv1	Adv2	Adv3	Adv4	Chr1
Monday		4	11	18	25	
Tuesday		5	12	19	26	
Wednesday		6	13	20	27	
Thursday		7	14	21	28	
Friday	1	8	15	22	29	
Saturday	2	9	16	23	30	

On Sunday 8 January the Epiphany may be celebrated, transferred from 6 January.

On Monday 9 January, the Baptism of Christ may be celebrated, if the Epiphany is celebrated on Sunday 8 January.

On Sunday 29 January the Presentation of Christ may be celebrated, transferred from 2 February.

On Sunday 5 November All Saints' Day may be celebrated, transferred from 1 November.